MW00637577

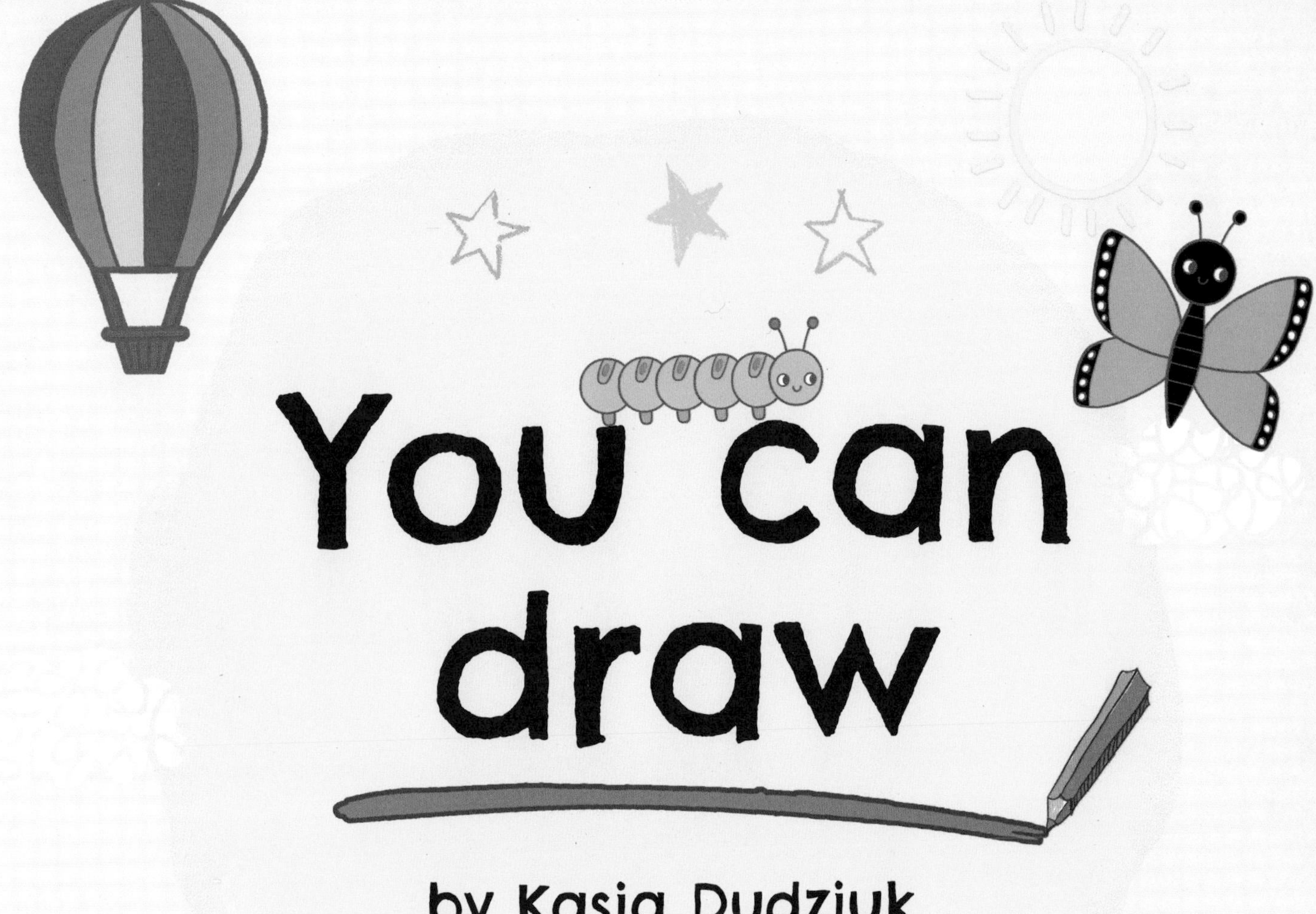

You can draw

by Kasia Dudziuk

This edition published in 2018 by Arcturus Publishing Limited
26/27 Bickels Yard, 151–153 Bermondsey Street,
London SE1 3HA

Written by JMS LLP
Illustrated by Kasia Dudziuk
Designed by Chris Bell

ISBN: 978-1-78888-304-7
CH005976NT
Supplier 29, Date 0918 Print run 6974

Printed in China

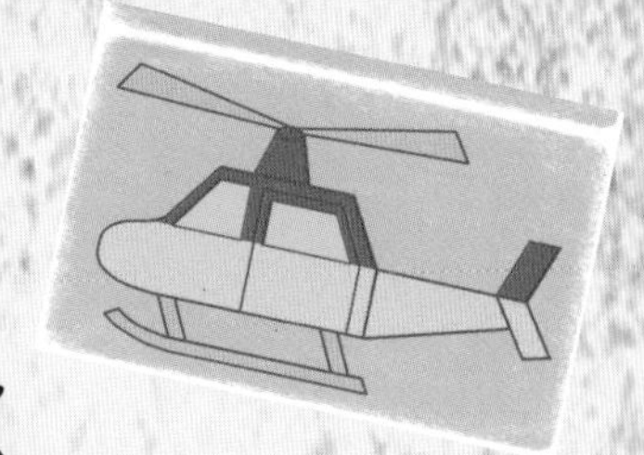

Contents

Wild Animals

Let's draw a zebra.

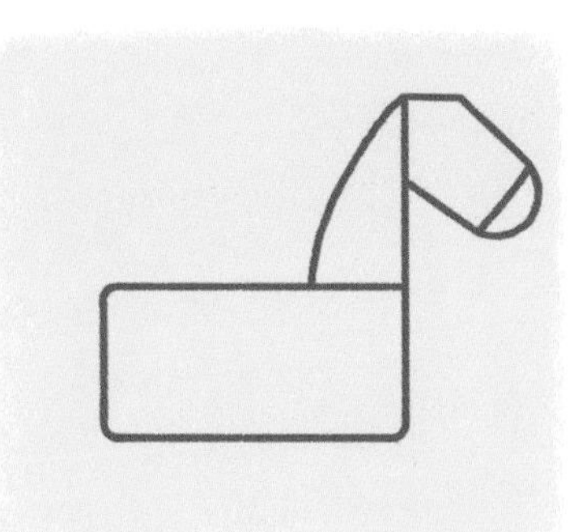

1 Here are his body and neck.

2 Now add his head and nose.

3 Don't forget his ears, legs, and long tail!

4 Give him a face and some black stripes.

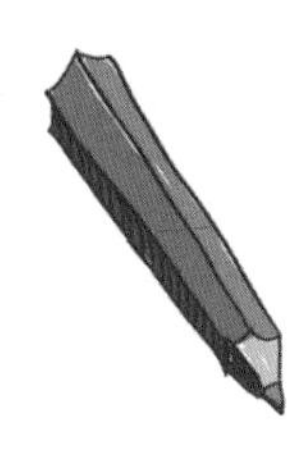

Try drawing some zebras here.

Draw a clever monkey.

1 She has a round head and big ears.

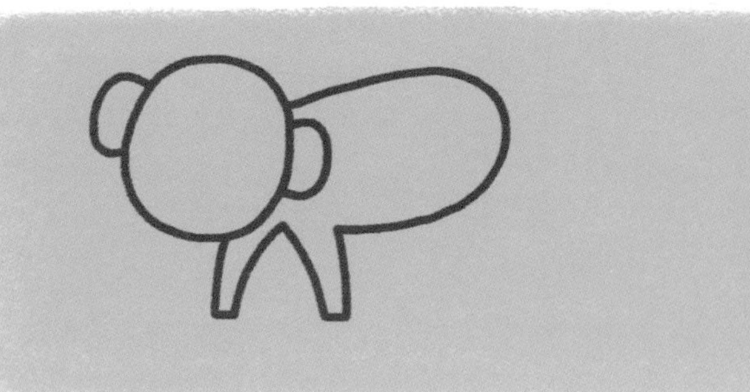

2 Add her body and front legs.

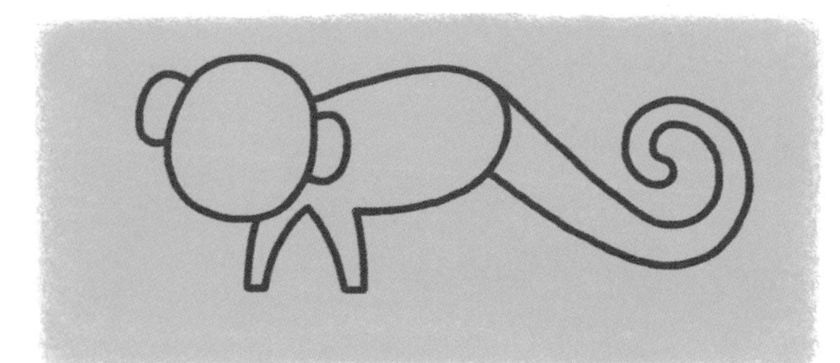

3 Now draw a long, curly tail, so she can swing through the trees!

4 Draw her back legs, face, and paws. Finish her in shades of brown.

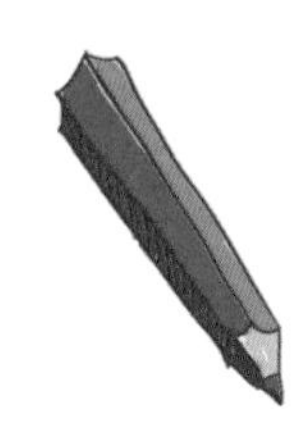

Draw your monkey here.

Draw some monkeys playing in the trees.

Draw a spotty jaguar.

1 Begin by drawing his round head and ears.

2 Add his front legs and paws.

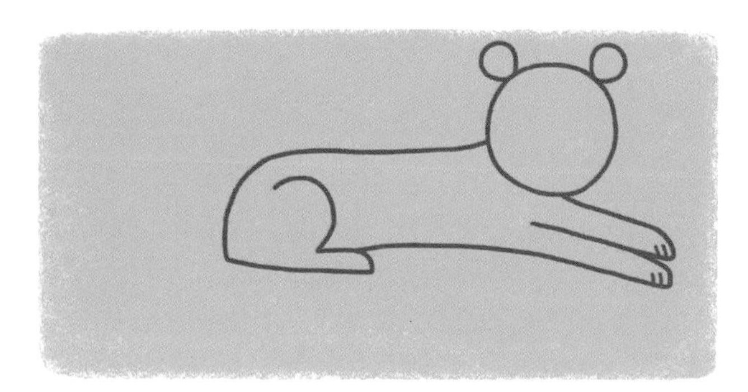

3 Now draw his body, and add a back leg.

4 Give him a curly tail, a happy face, and some little black spots.

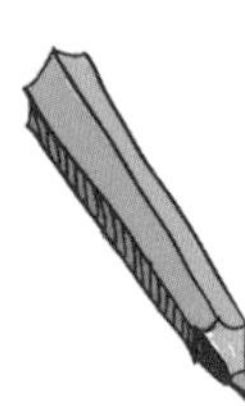

Try drawing a jaguar here.

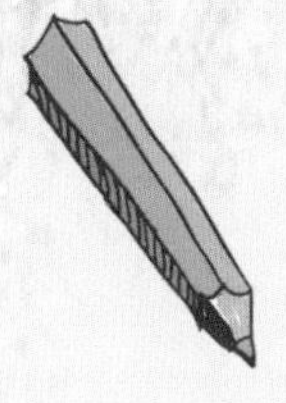

Draw some jaguars in different positions ...

This jaguar is sitting down.

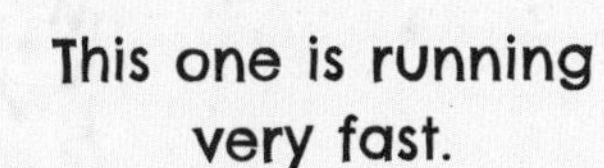

This one is running very fast.

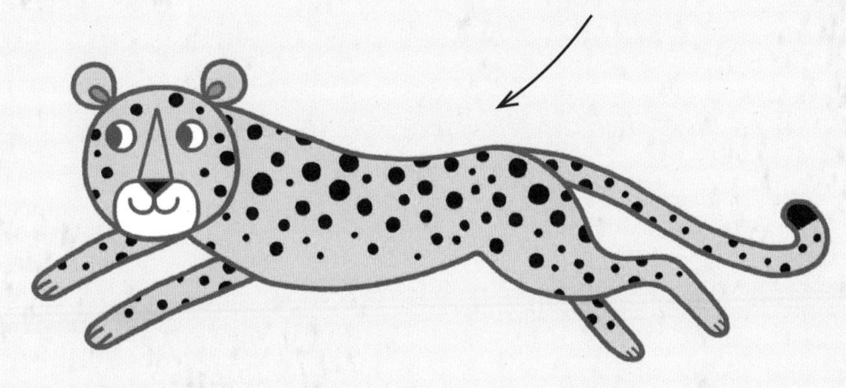

... or even a panther!

A jaguar with black fur is called a panther.

Can you draw a porcupine?

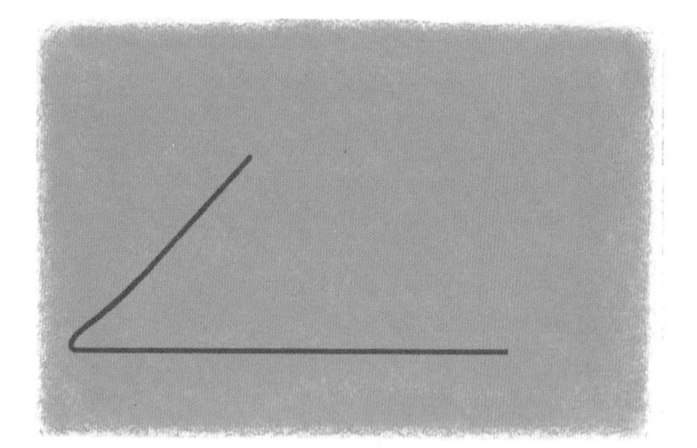

1 Draw two lines like this for her snout.

2 Now draw lots of spines on her back.

3 Add four little legs under her tummy.

4 Draw her face and whiskers. She is all brown except for a little pink nose.

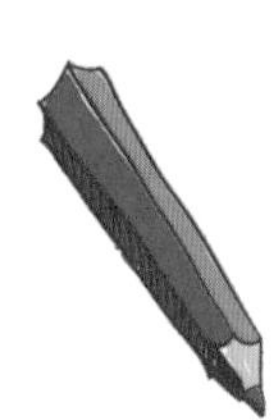

Now it's your turn ...

How about a rhinoceros?

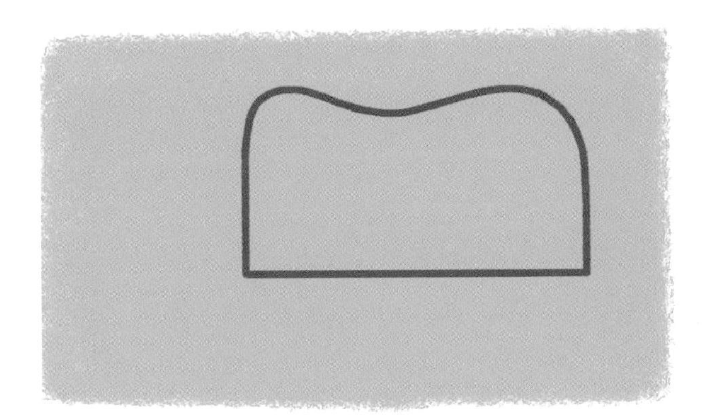

1 First draw this shape for his body.

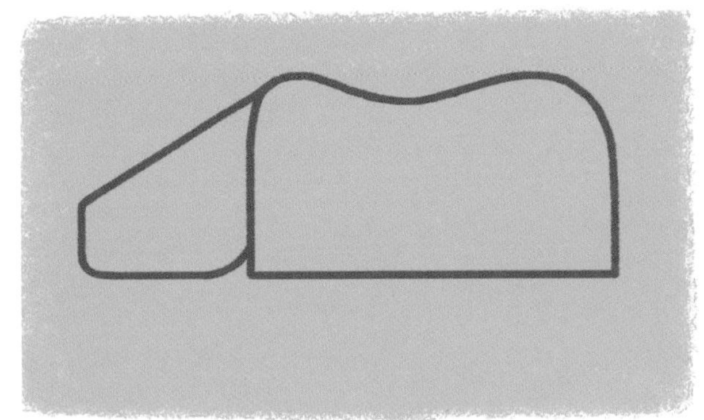

2 Add his head at the front.

3 Give him four strong legs and a little tail.

4 Add his face, tiny ears, and two white horns on his nose. Don't forget his toes!

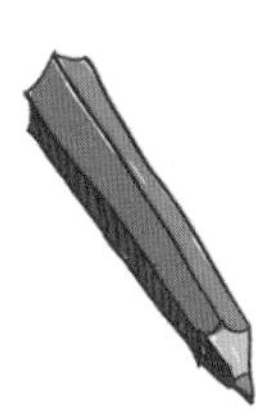

Draw your rhinoceros here.

Let's try a chameleon.

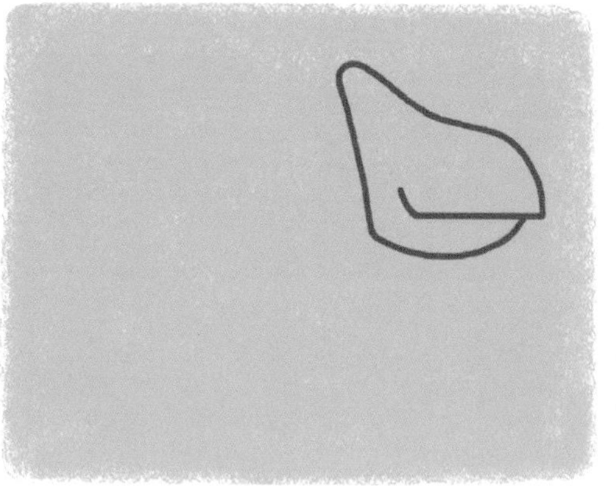

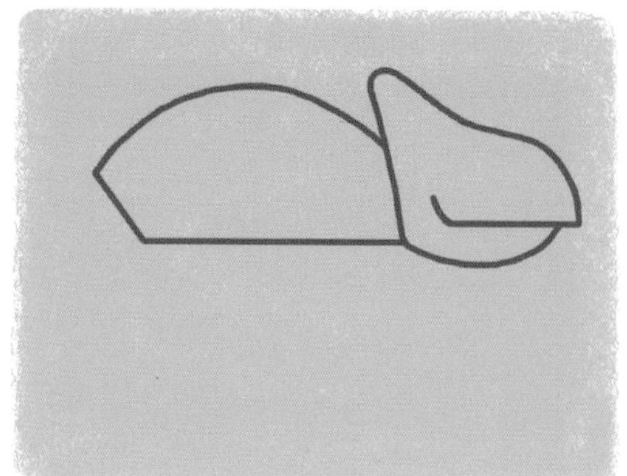

1 Begin with this wiggly shape for her head.

2 The top of her body is curved, but the bottom is straight.

3 She needs four little legs.

4 Add her long tail and a big, round eye. Give her orange and green stripes.

Try drawing a chameleon here.

Chameleons can use camouflage ...

... to hide just about anywhere!

This chameleon is blue and yellow.

This one is lime green and red.

Why not try a pink and purple striped one?

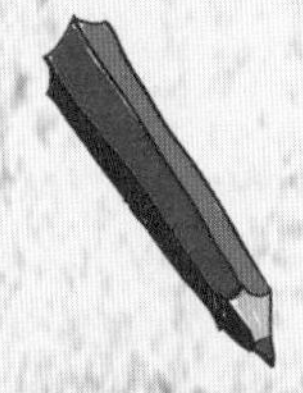

Now draw your own cool chameleons!

Learn to draw a flamingo!

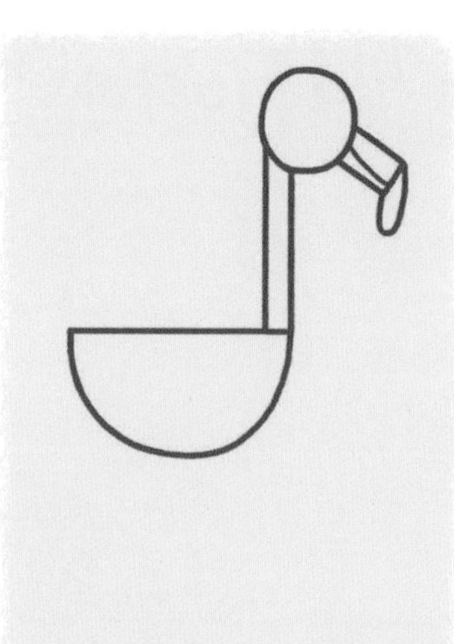

1 Begin with her round head and long neck.

2 Then draw a half circle for her body and add her beak.

3 Give her two thin legs. She likes to stand on just one!

4 Draw her curved beak, eye, and wing. Flamingos are bright pink!

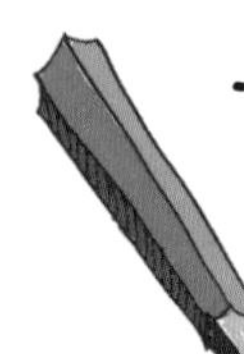

Try drawing a flamingo.

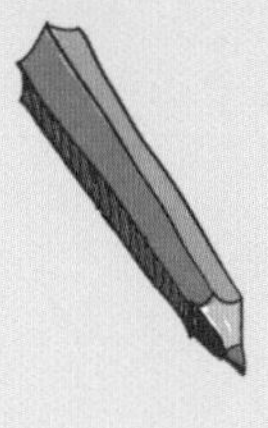

Draw a flock of flamingos in the water.

Let's draw a wildebeest!

1 First draw her head, snout, and horns.

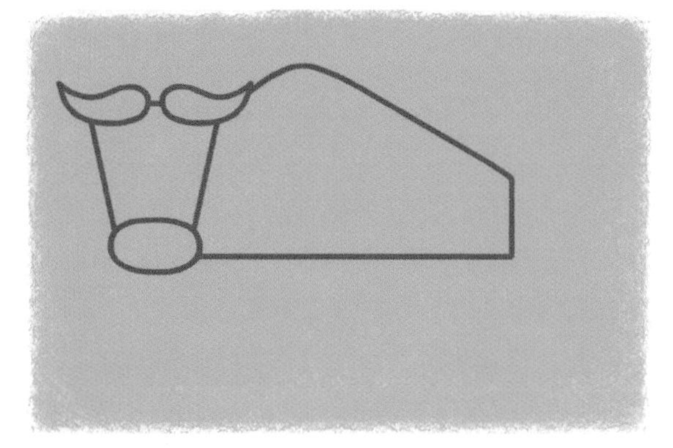

2 Then draw this shape for her body.

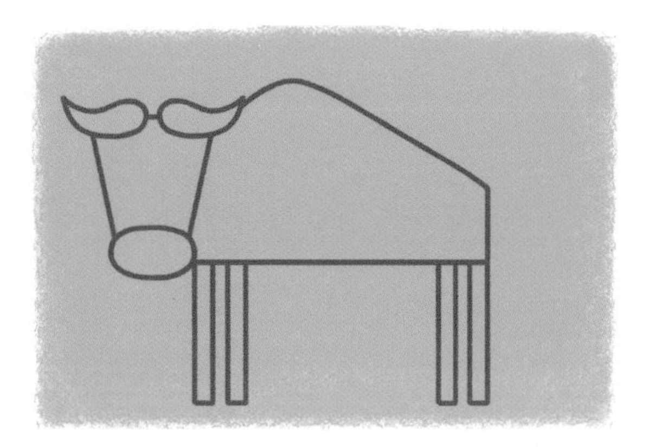

3 She has long, thin legs.

4 Add her face, mane, toes, and tail. Use different shades of brown.

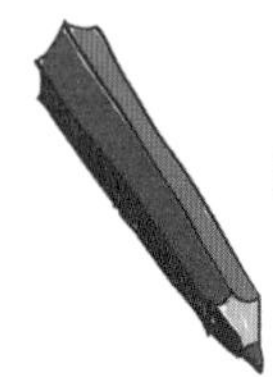

Can you draw a wildebeest?

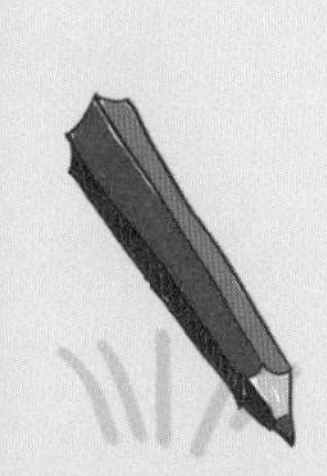

Draw some wildebeest out on the plain.

How about a little tree frog?

1 Start with his head and big, round eyes.

2 Now he needs front legs and a body.

3 He has big, strong back legs for jumping!

4 Add his eyes and mouth, and make him bright green.

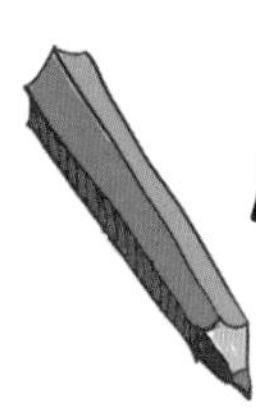

Now it's your turn to try ...

Now try a big, hairy gorilla!

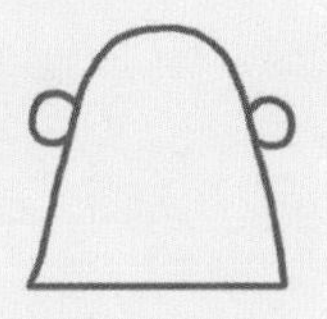

1 First draw his head and little ears.

2 Add his big arms. They are very strong!

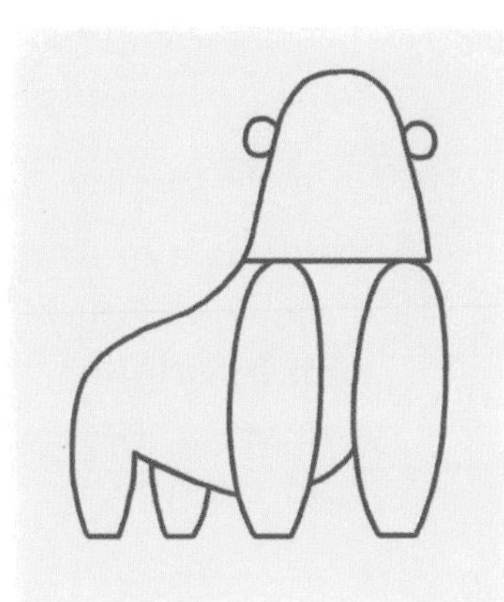

3 Draw this shape for his body and legs.

4 Give him a smiley face, pink paws, and black fur.

Draw a gorilla here.

Draw a pretty lovebird.

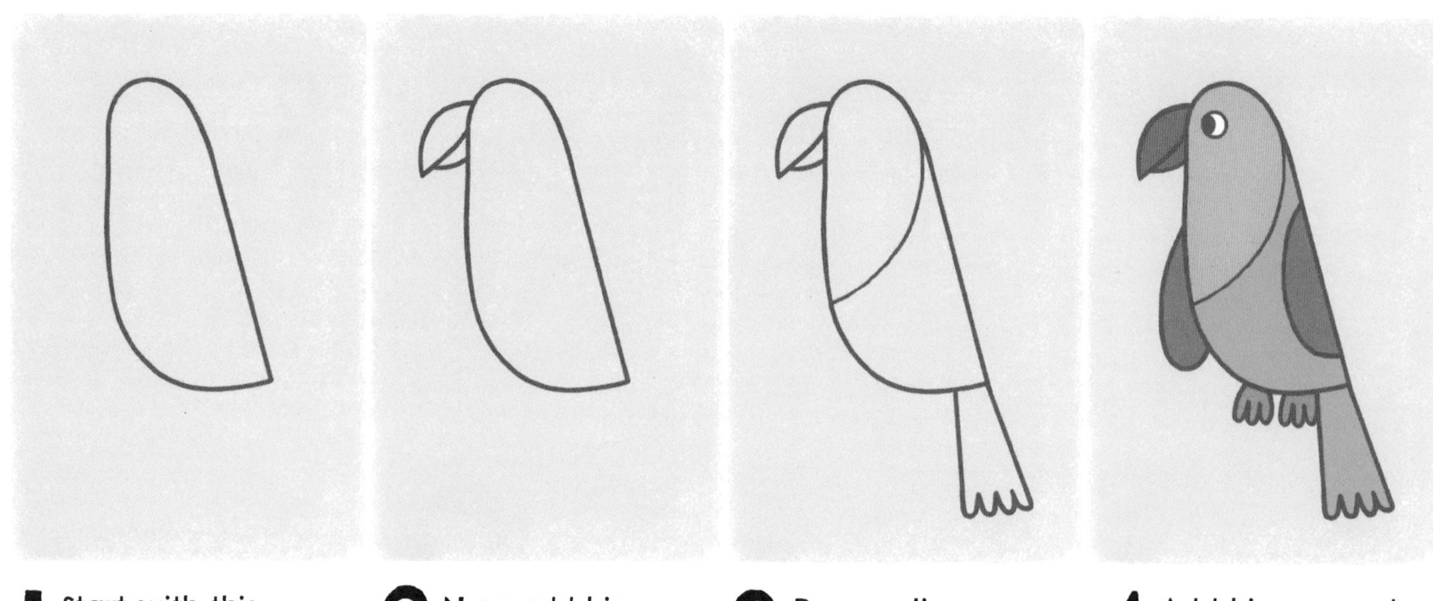

1 Start with this shape for his body.

2 Now add his beak.

3 Draw a line across his chest, and add his tail.

4 Add his eye and little feet. Finish him in bright shades of green and orange.

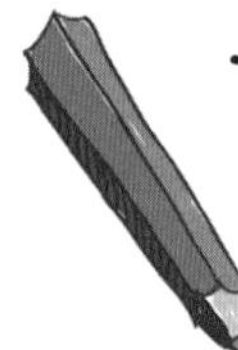

Try drawing some lovebirds here.
They always come in pairs!

Can you draw the birds that laid these eggs?

Draw an elegant gazelle.

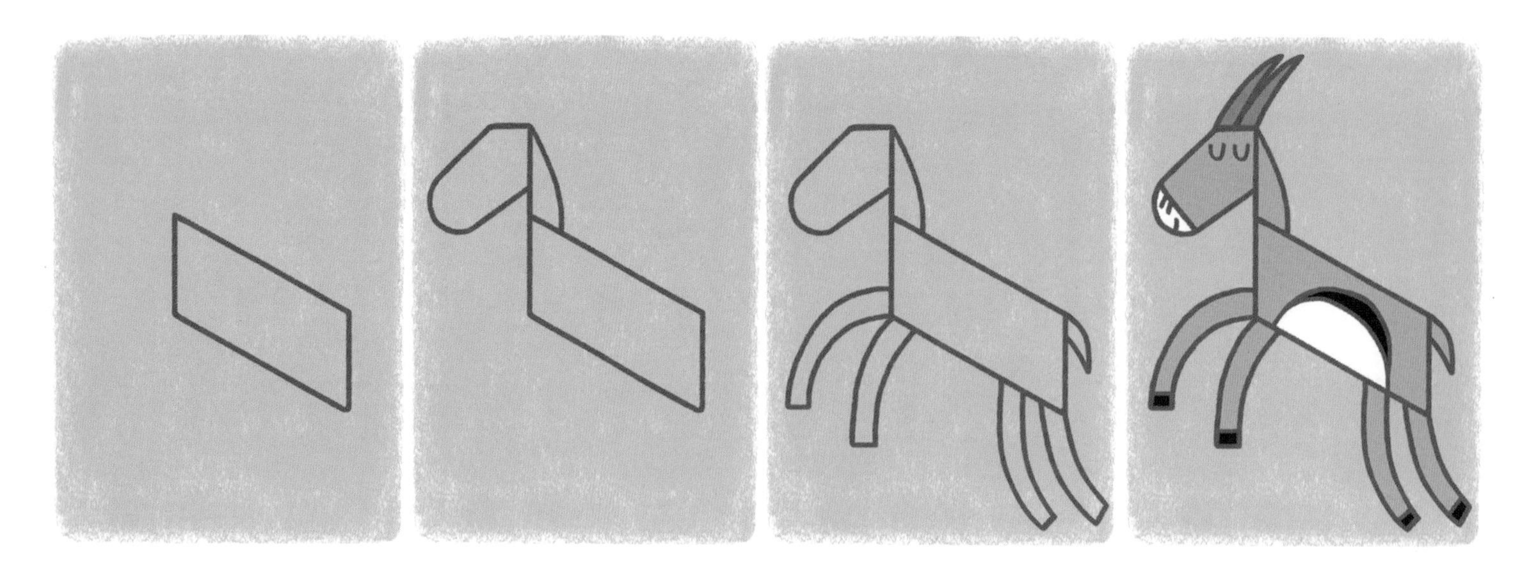

1 Draw this shape for his body.

2 Now he has a head and neck.

3 He needs legs and a tail!

4 Add his horns and face, and shade him in.

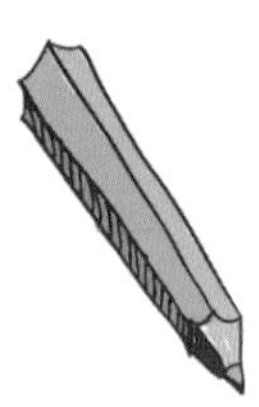

Now you can try.

Draw some gazelles leaping across the savannah.

How about a tall giraffe?

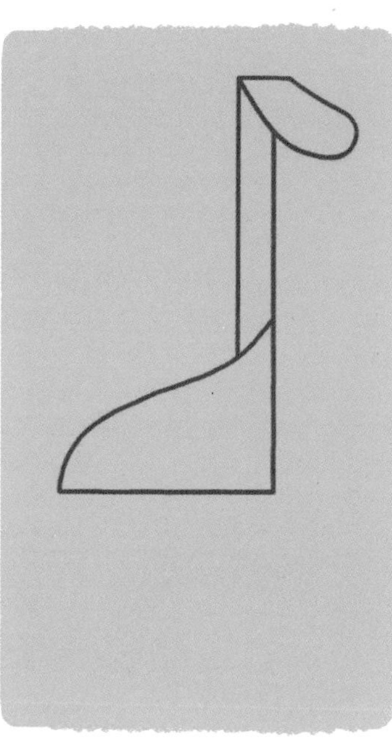

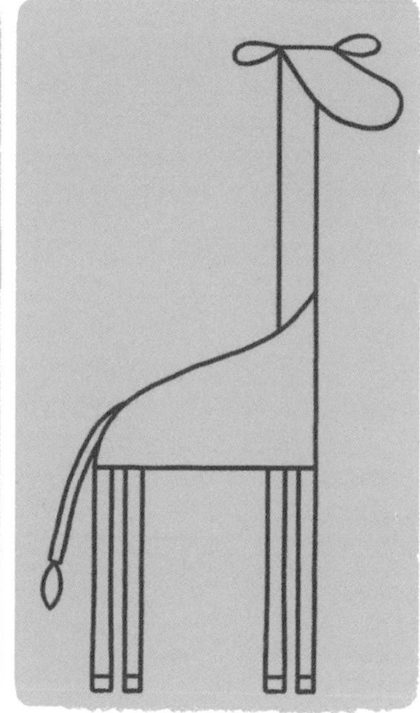

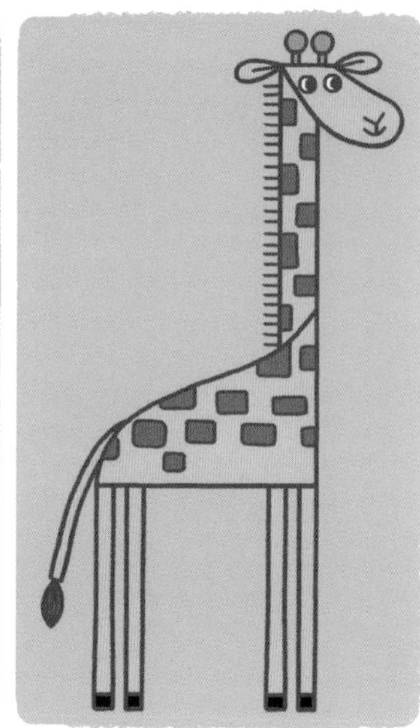

1 First, draw this shape for his body.

2 Add his head and long neck.

3 He has long legs and a tail as well!

4 Give him a face, horns, and some pretty spots.

Draw a few giraffes here.

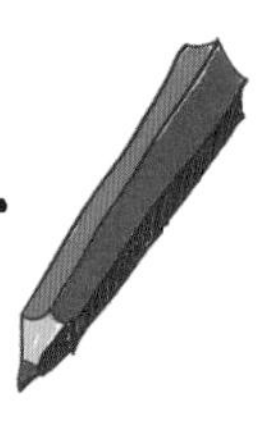

Draw some giraffes eating from the treetops.

Let's draw an elephant.

1 Here's her body.

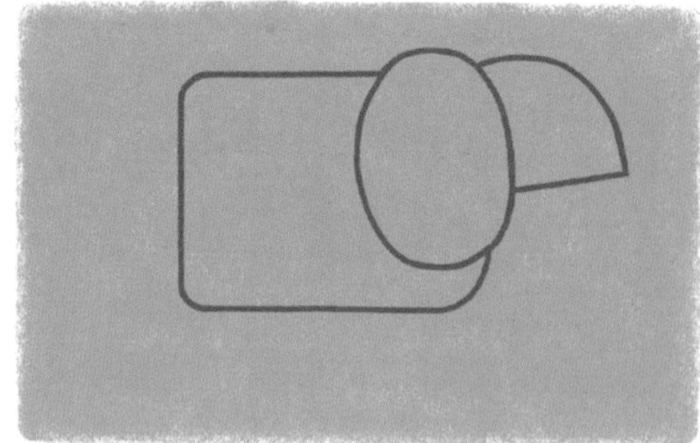

2 Give her a head and a big ear.

3 Add her curly trunk, thick legs, and tail.

4 Add her face, tusks, trunk, and toes, then shade her in. She looks very happy, doesn't she?

Try drawing your own elephant!

Draw a line of elephants with a baby at the back.

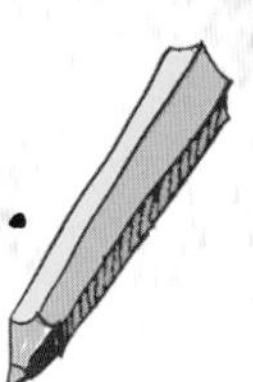

Now let's try a python.

1 Start with a semicircle for the python's head and her long neck.

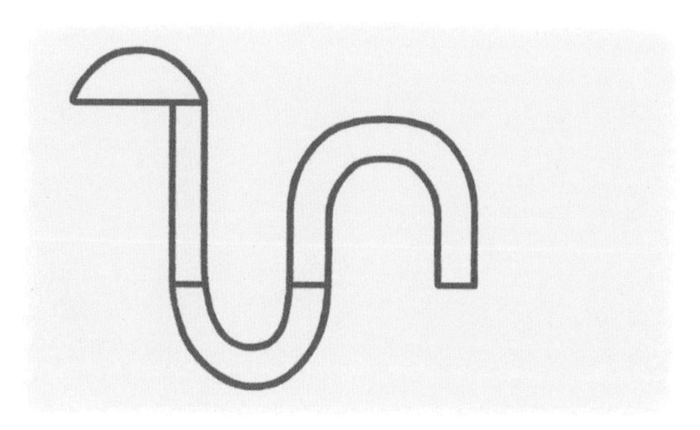

2 Add two U-shapes to make coils for her body ...

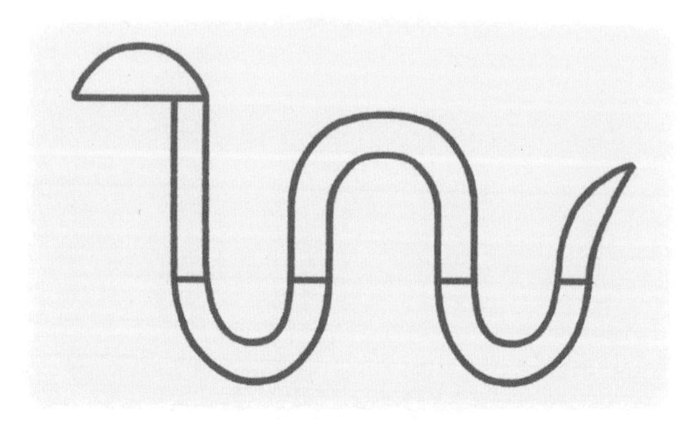

3 ... and another coil, before finishing with the tip of her tail.

4 Give her an eye and a forked tongue. Add a zigzag pattern to her body and make her different shades of green.

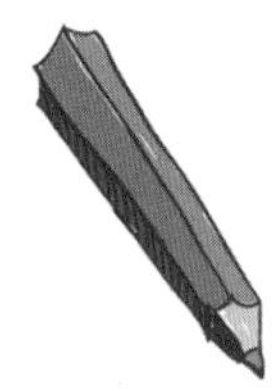

Try drawing some pythons here.

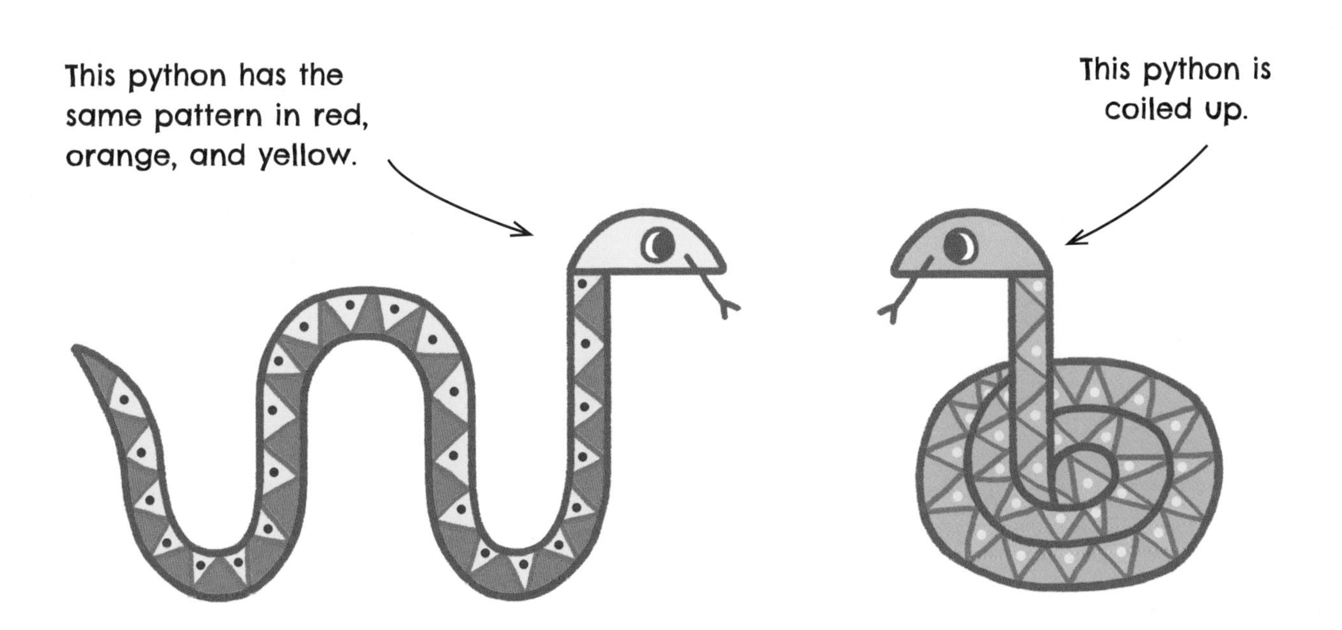

Can you draw a coiled python?

Can you draw a lion?

1 Draw his head and mane.

2 Add his body.

3 He needs legs and a tail!

4 Draw his face. He has an orange mane.

Now it's your turn.

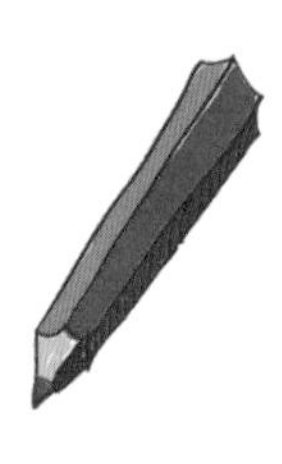

Draw a pretty parrot.

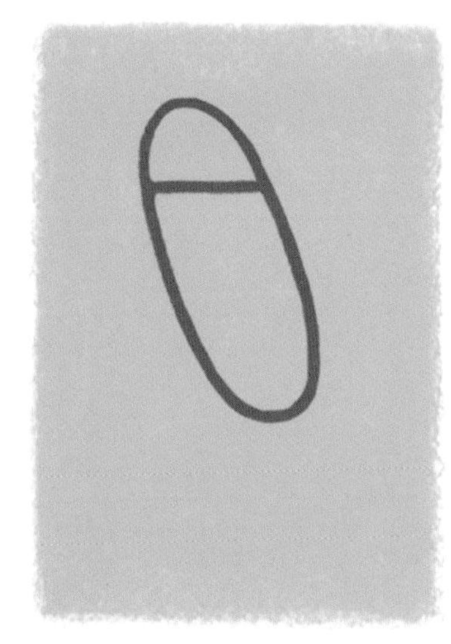

1 Draw her body and head.

2 Now she has a beak and feet.

3 She needs wings and feathers!

4 Add her eye and tail. Her feathers are red, yellow, and green!

Now you have a try.

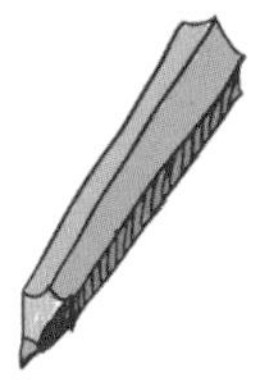

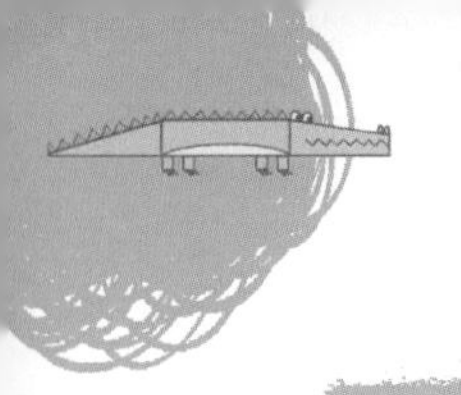

Now let's try a crocodile.

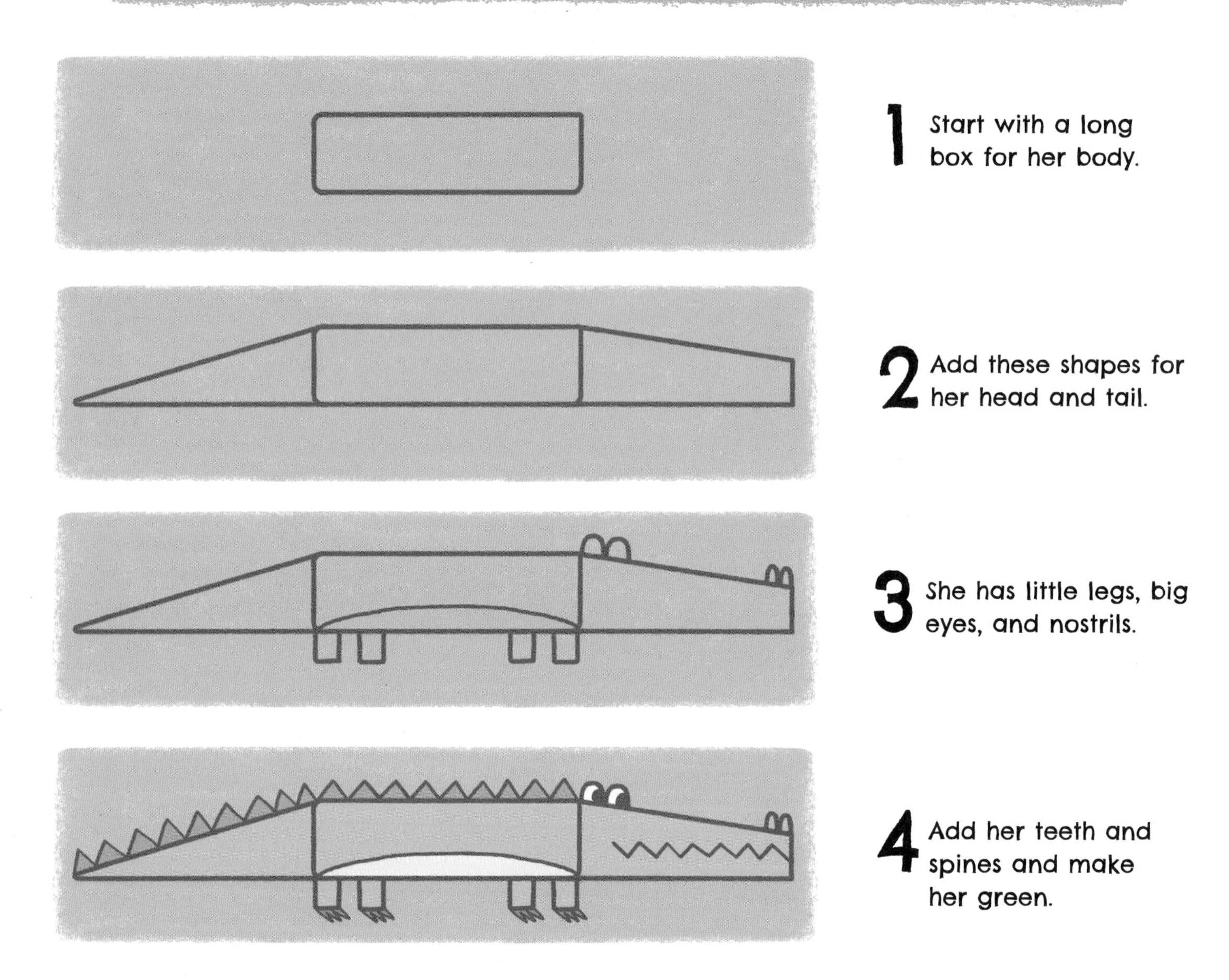

1 Start with a long box for her body.

2 Add these shapes for her head and tail.

3 She has little legs, big eyes, and nostrils.

4 Add her teeth and spines and make her green.

This is how you show her swimming in the water.

Draw some crocodiles in the river.

Can you draw an anteater?

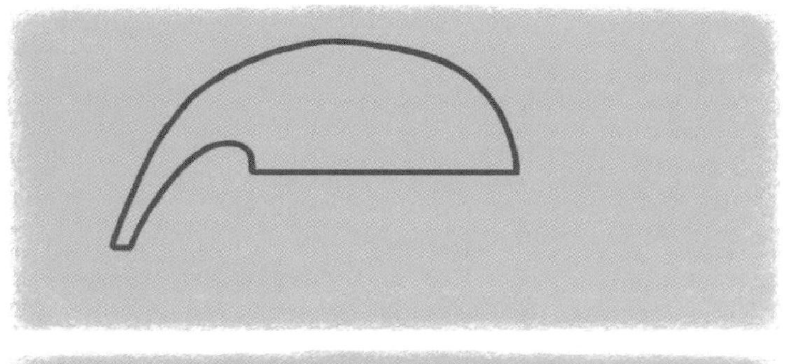

1 Here's her body and long snout.

2 Now add her four little legs.

3 Add her long, thick tail.

4 Give her an eye, ears, feet, and a long, curly tongue. It's perfect for licking up all those ants!

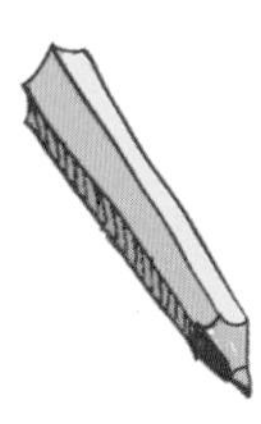

Try drawing an anteater here. →

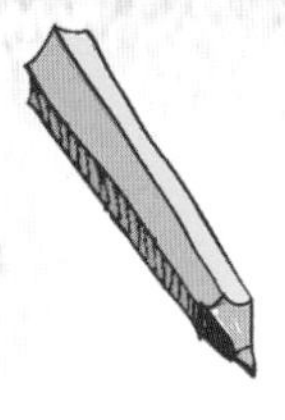

Draw an anteater to slurp up these ants!

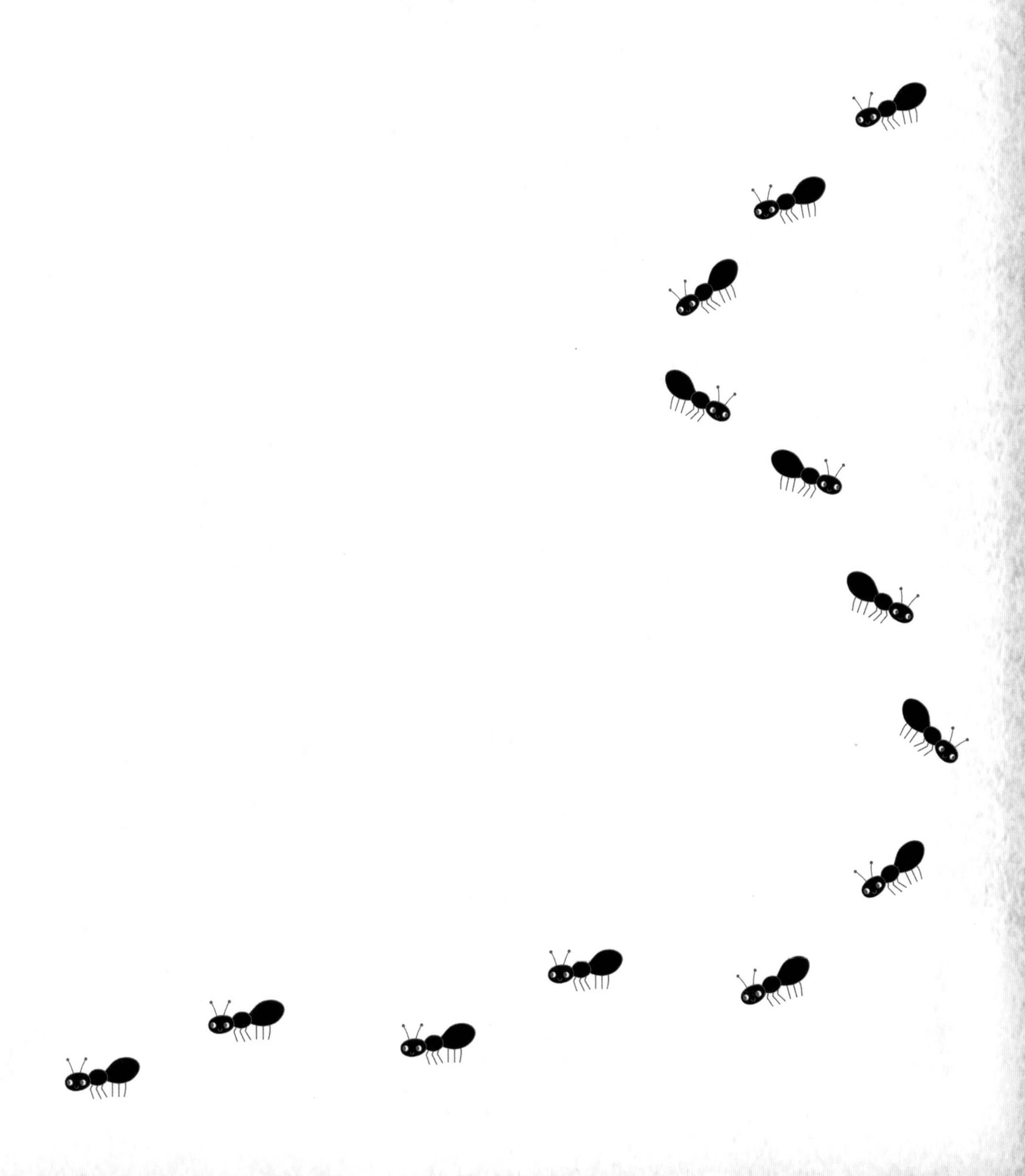

Try drawing a penguin.

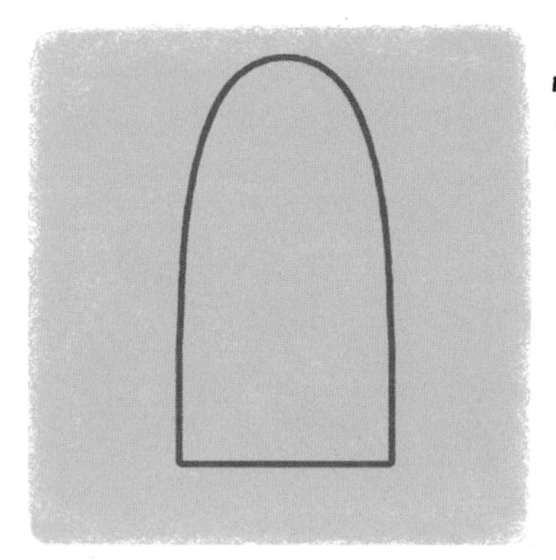

1 First draw this shape for her head and body.

2 Draw a curved line across her chest for her head.

3 Give her wings and little feet.

4 Add her eyes and yellow beak. Then make her black and white, with orange feet. She's finished!

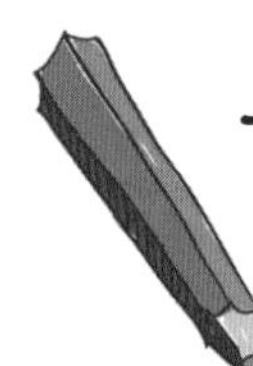

Try drawing a penguin here.

You can also draw a baby penguin!

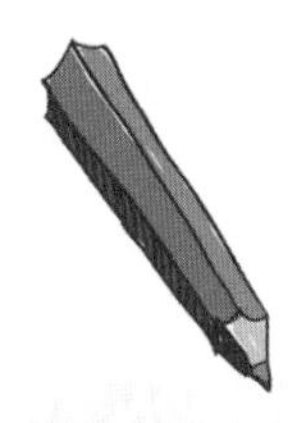

Can you draw a family of penguins?

Draw a hippopotamus!

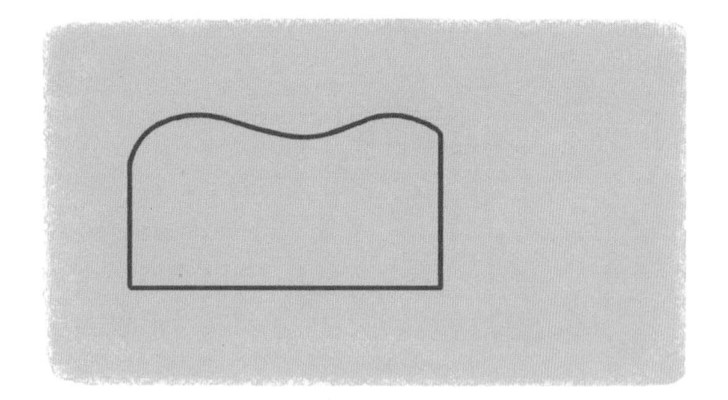

1 Begin by drawing this shape for his body.

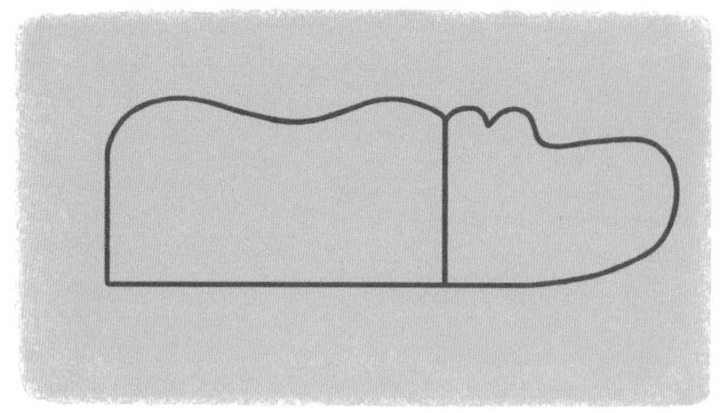

2 Now draw his head. It's very big, isn't it?

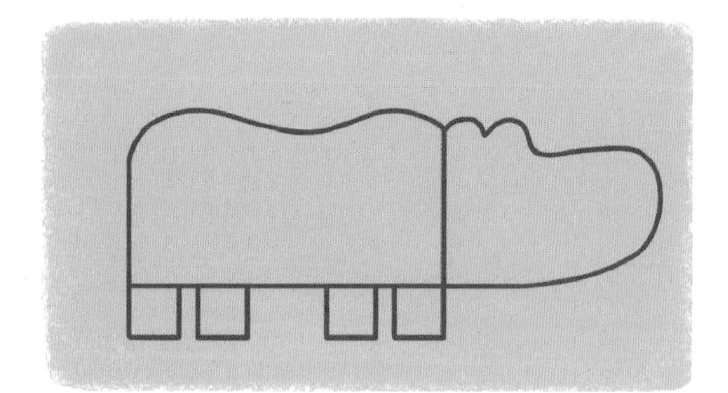

3 He has four short, strong legs.

4 Add his face, ears, tail, and toes. Give him a happy smile.

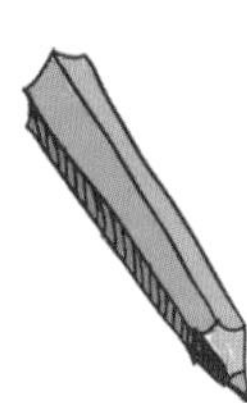

Try drawing a hippo here.

Draw some hippos cooling off in the mud!

Learn to draw a toucan.

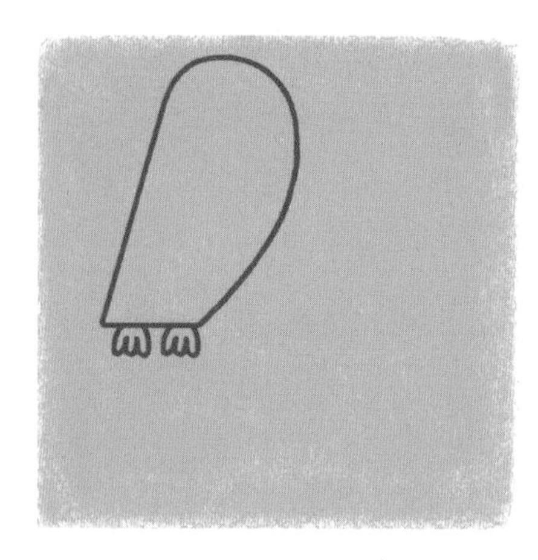

1 Draw this shape for his body, and add his little feet.

2 He needs a very big beak!

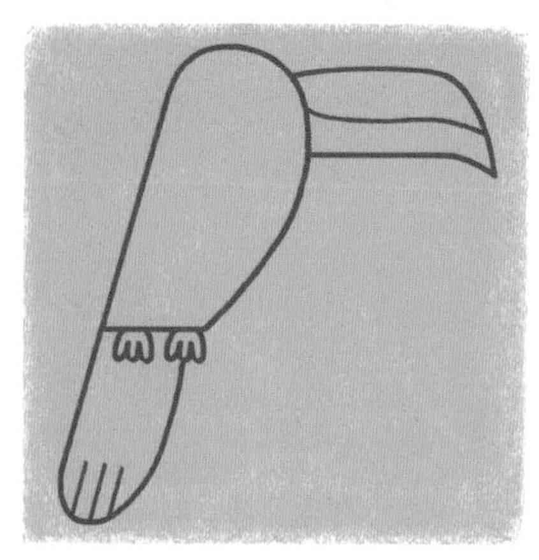

3 Add his long tail feathers.

4 Give him a beady eye. Make his feathers black and white, and his beak red and orange.

Now you can try ...

Let's try a scarlet macaw.

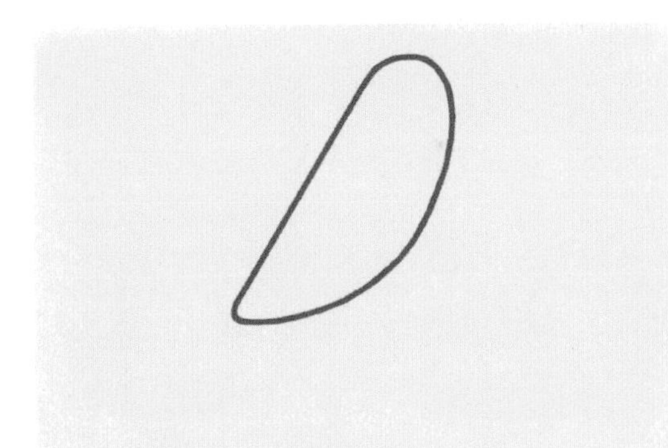

1 Start by drawing this shape for her body.

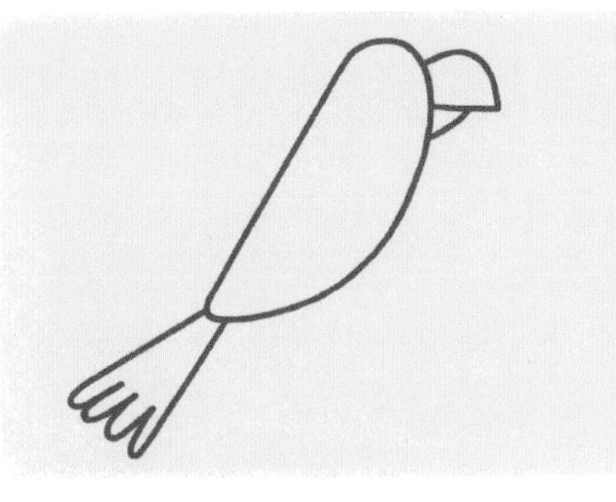

2 Now add her beak and tail feathers.

3 Draw her wings stretched out in flight.

4 Add her eyes and feet. Her feathers are bright red.

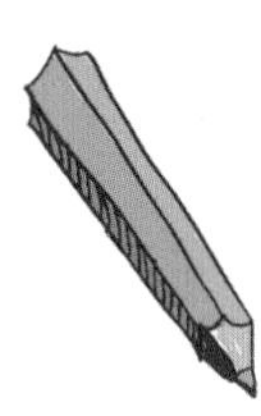

Draw your own macaw here.

Under the Sea

Draw a deep-sea diver

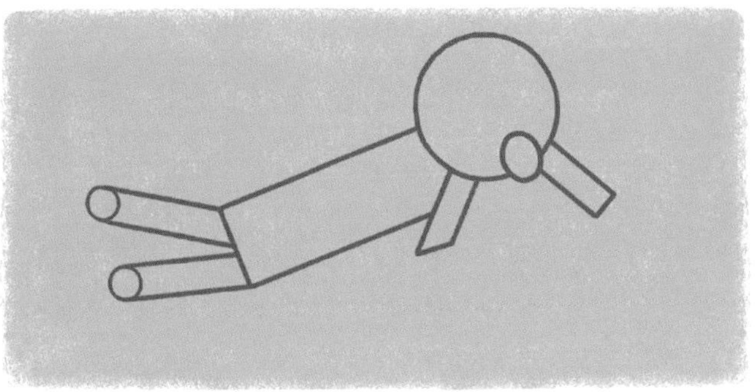

1 Start with her head and body.

2 Then draw some shapes for her arms and legs.

3 Finish her arms. She needs flippers, a mask, and an air tank!

4 Add her hands and eyes. Shade her in and don't forget her breathing tube!

Can you draw a diver here?

Try drawing a seahorse.

1 Begin by drawing his head.

2 Then draw his body.

3 He has a cute, curly tail.

4 He needs a fin and a crown. Add his face and lines on his tummy!

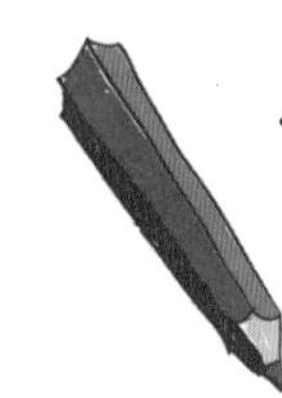

Try drawing a seahorse here.

Seahorses are really fish!

Learn to draw a dolphin ...

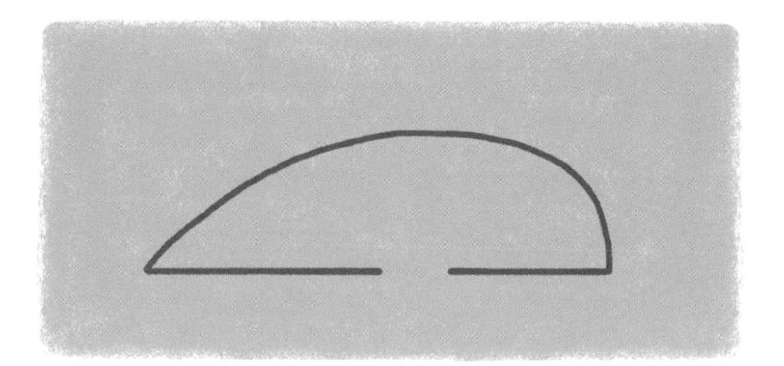

1 Start with a simple semi-circle shape for her body.

2 Add some fins to help her swim.

3 Draw her tail and a long nose.

4 Add her smiley face and shade her in. Now she's ready for a swim!

Try drawing a dolphin here.

... and a whale!

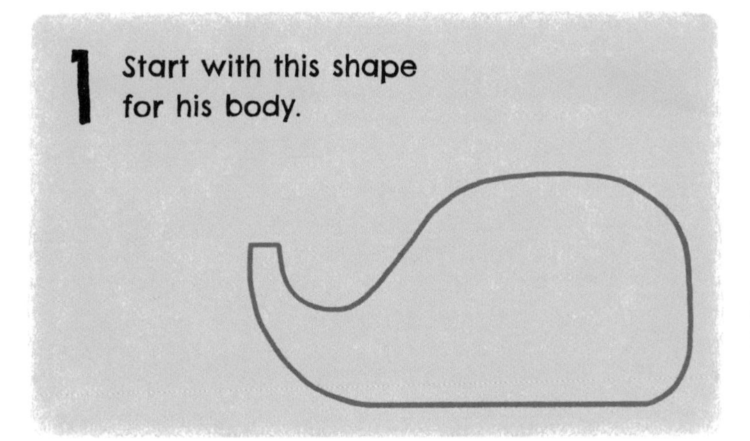

1 Start with this shape for his body.

2 Now draw his tail.

3 Don't forget his waterspout!

4 Make him blue and give him a friendly face.

Now draw a whale.

What about an octopus?

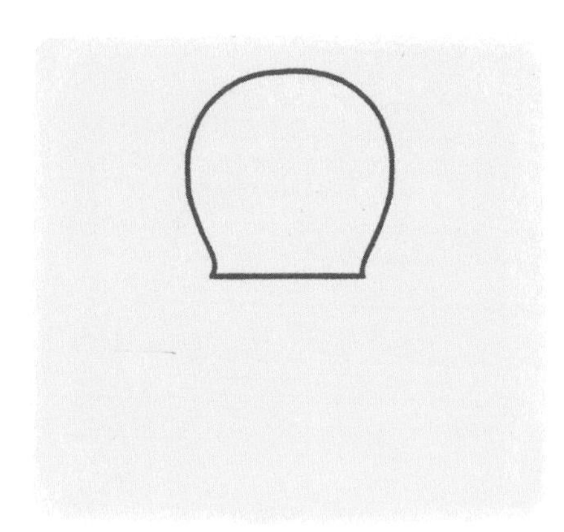

1 Start with his head.

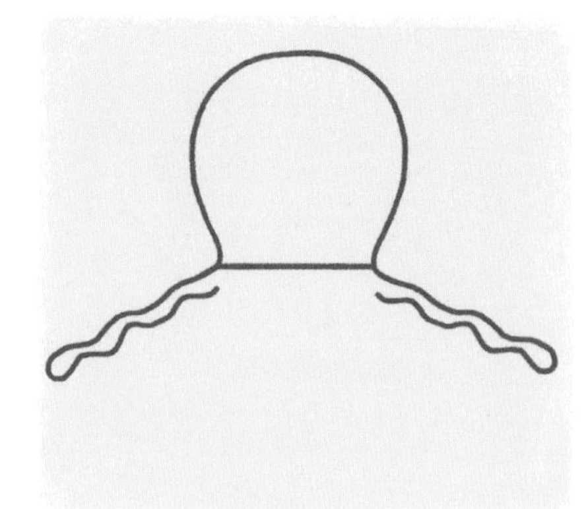

2 Draw his two outer legs.

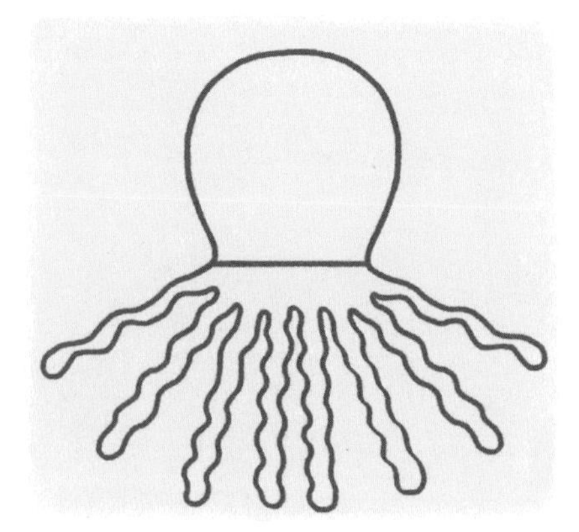

3 He needs six more legs!

4 Give him a smiley face and make him bright orange!

Now you have a try.

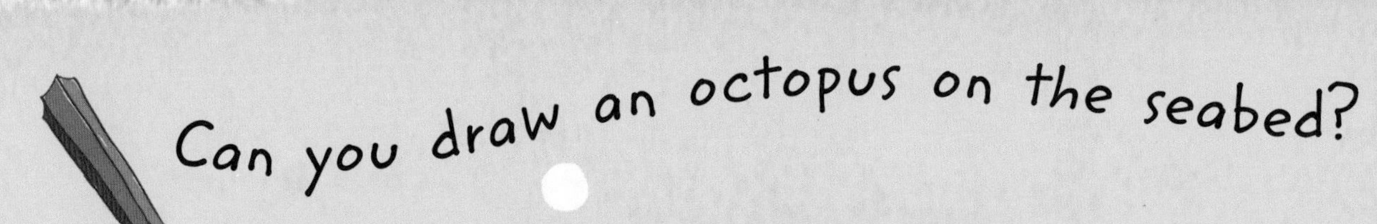
Can you draw an octopus on the seabed?

Let's try a lobster!

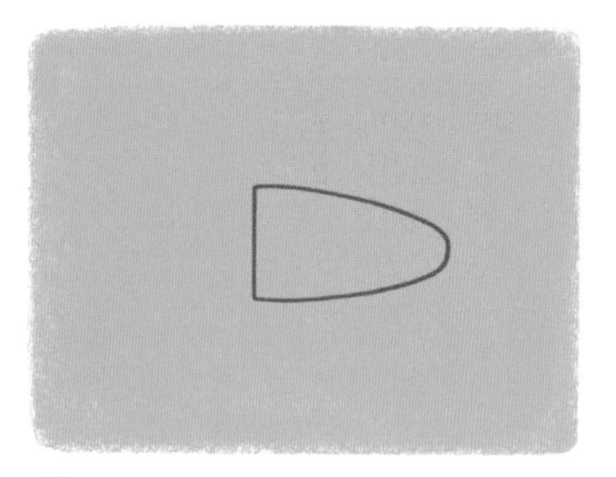

1 First draw this shape for his head and body.

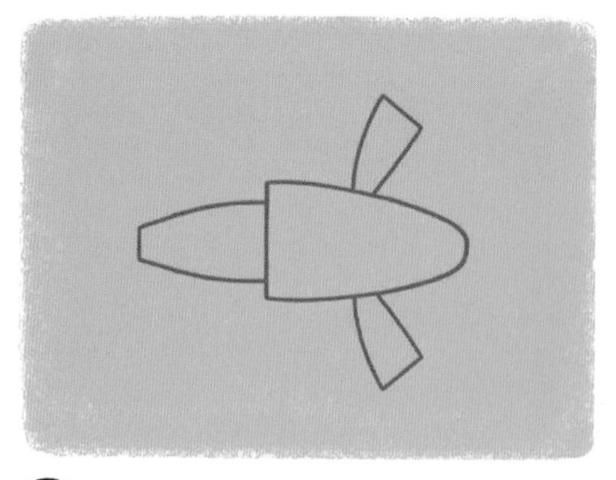

2 Add his front legs and his tail.

3 Draw his pincer claws and his tail fin.

4 Add his eyes, legs, and antennae. He is bright red!

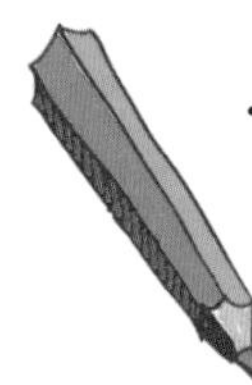

Try drawing a lobster here.

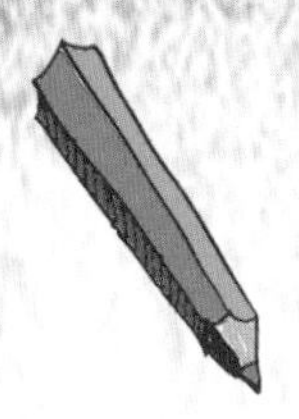

Can you draw a hermit crab?

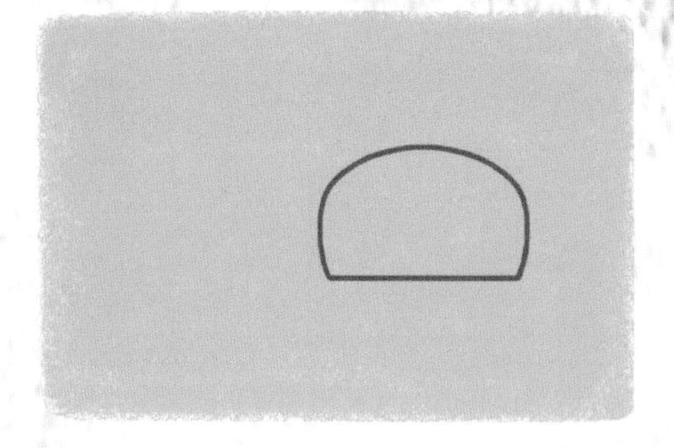

1 First draw this shape for her body.

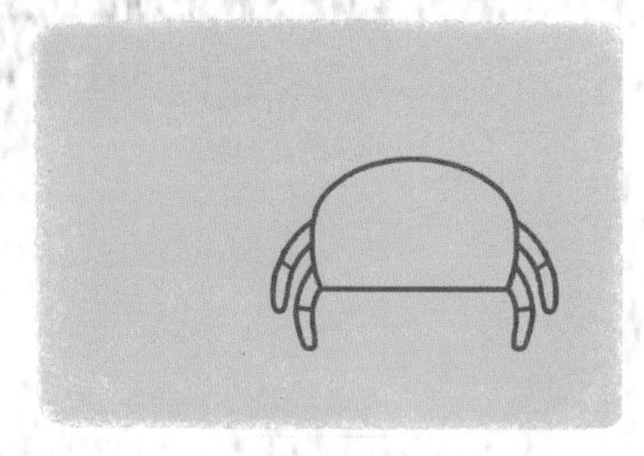

2 Next add four little legs.

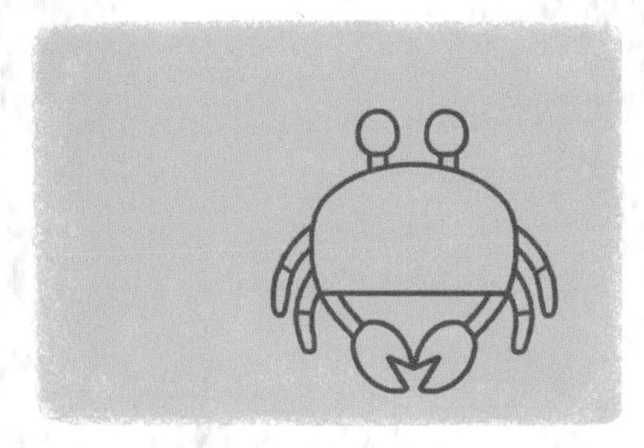

3 Add her eyes and then her front legs and claws.

4 Add her bumpy shell, and give her an orange face.

Hermit crabs use old shells as their homes.

Draw a super starfish.

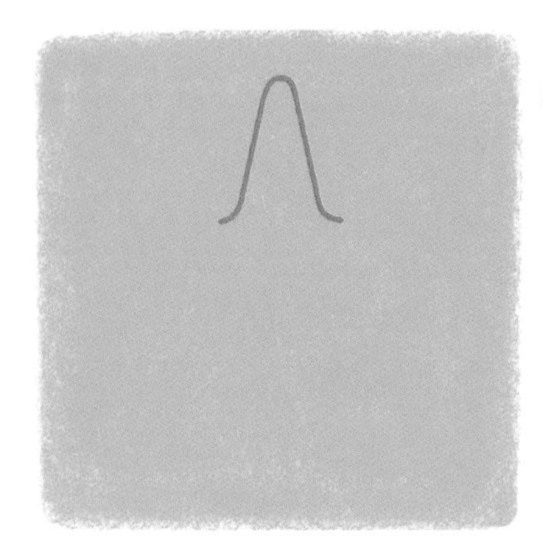

1 Start with the arm at the top of the starfish.

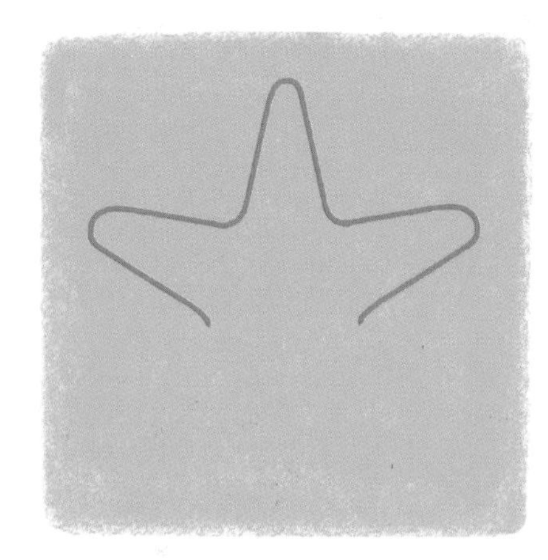

2 Add the two side arms ...

3 ... and the two arms at the bottom.

4 Give him a happy face, and make him a lovely shade of orange.

Try drawing a starfish here.

Starfish come in lots of different shapes and sizes!

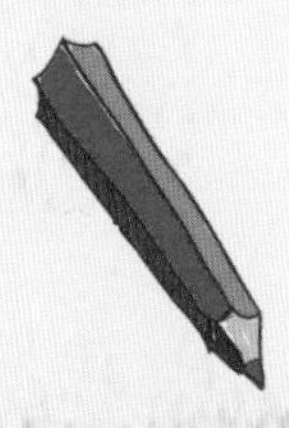

How many different starfish can you draw?

How about a jellyfish?

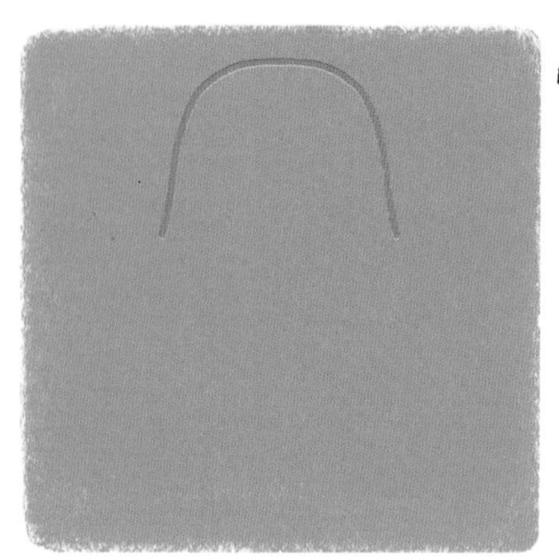

1 First draw this shape for her head.

2 Draw the bottom of her head with a wavy edge.

3 Add six long wiggly lines for her arms.

4 Draw her cute face, and finish her in a pretty shade of pink.

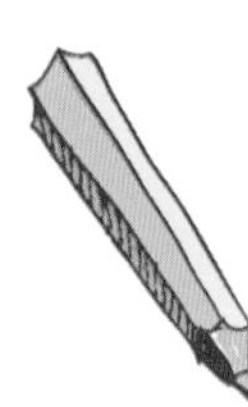

Draw your own jellyfish ...

Now let's draw a walrus.

1 Draw this shape for his head and chest. Add his flippers.

2 Give him a nice, big mouth.

3 Draw his body and his two long tusks.

4 Finish his face, and give him a tail. Don't forget his whiskers!

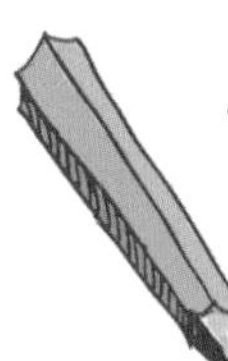

Try drawing a walrus here.

Now try a shark!

1 First draw this shape for her body.

2 Next, draw in some fins.

3 She needs a tail and a smiley mouth.

4 Don't forget her face and those sharp teeth when you shade her in!

Not all sharks look so happy!

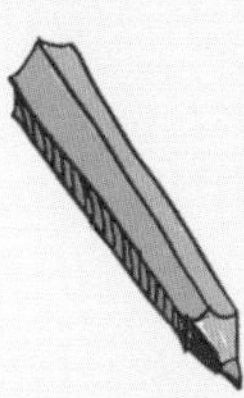

Can you draw some sharks in the water?

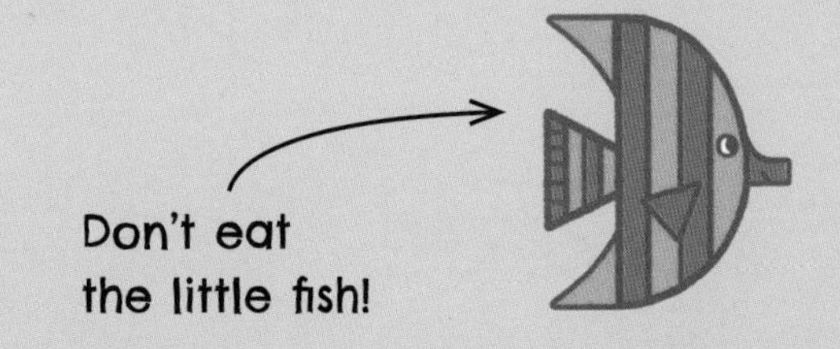

Let's draw a tropical fish!

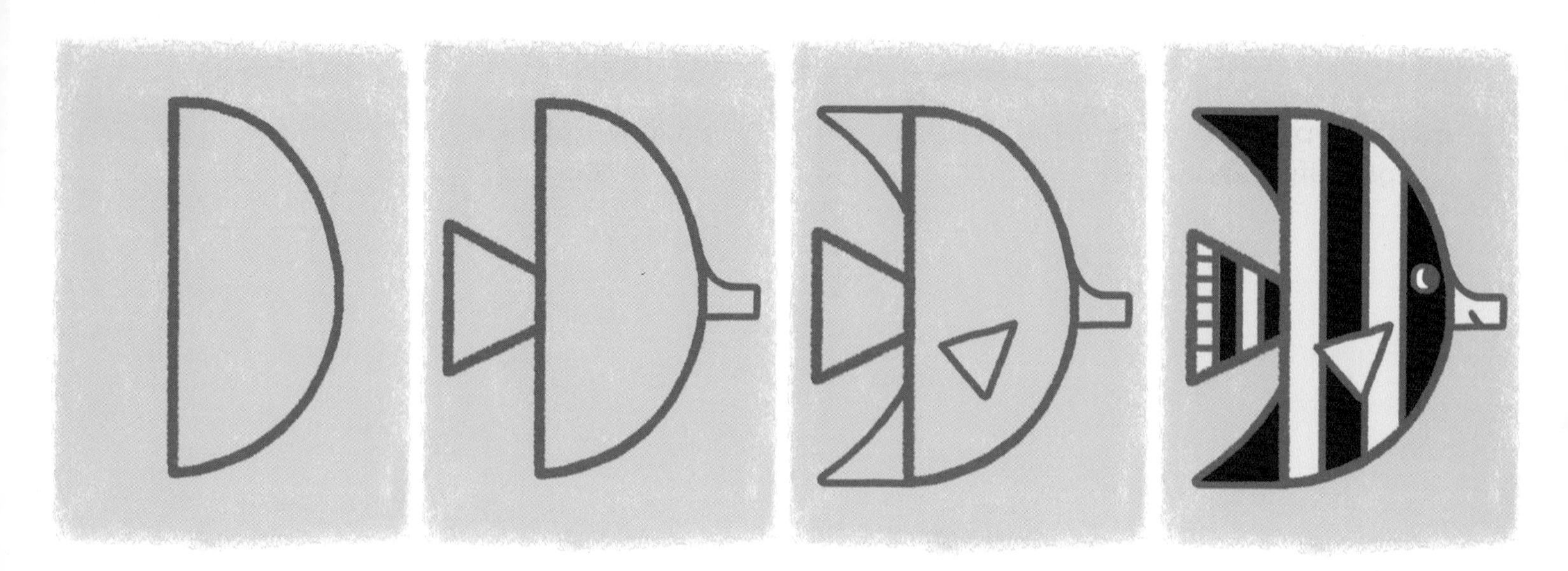

1 Start with his body shape.

2 Add his nose and tail.

3 He needs fins to help him swim.

4 Give him some bright stripes!

Now draw your own little fish.

Let's try an oyster.

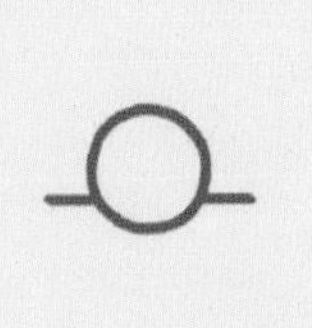

1 First draw the round pearl and a line for the hinge of the shell.

2 Draw the top and bottom of the shell with wavy edges.

3 Add a curved line around the edges to finish the oyster.

4 Draw the ridges of the shell, and finish in pale shades with a white pearl.

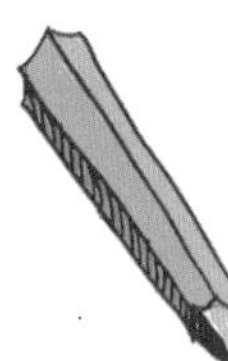

Try drawing an oyster here.

Learn to draw a narwhal!

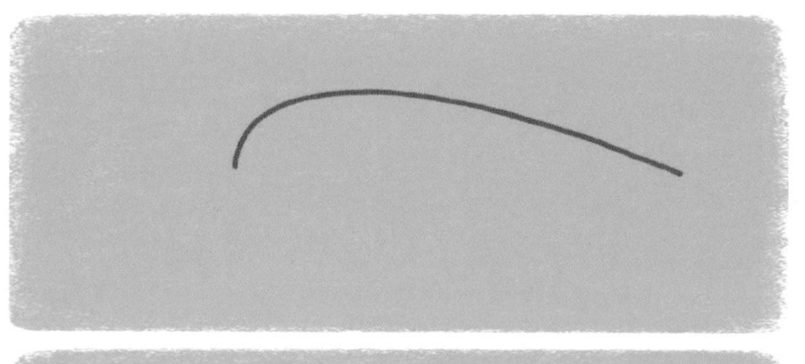

1 First draw a curved line to make her back.

2 Then draw another curved line for her tummy. Add her flipper.

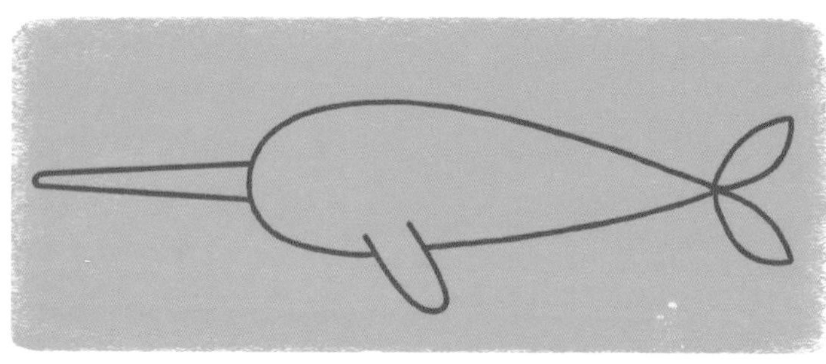

3 Add her long, pointed horn and her tail fins.

4 Give her a happy face, and draw some lines on her horn. She is dark blue, like the deep sea.

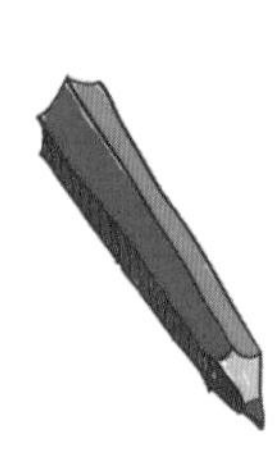

Try drawing a narwhal here. →

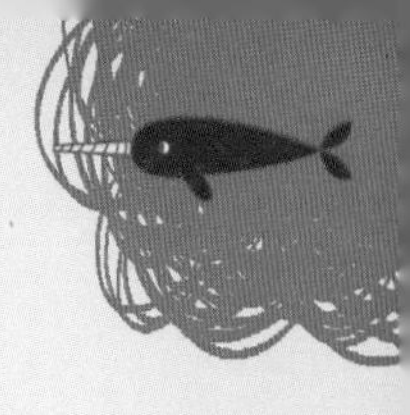

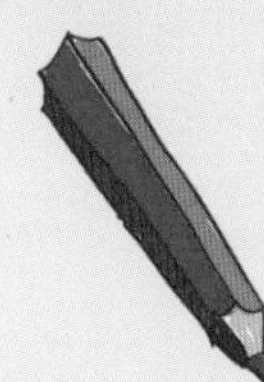

Draw a narwhal diving in the ocean.

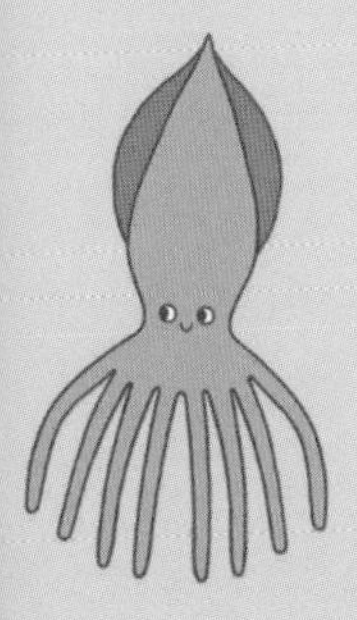

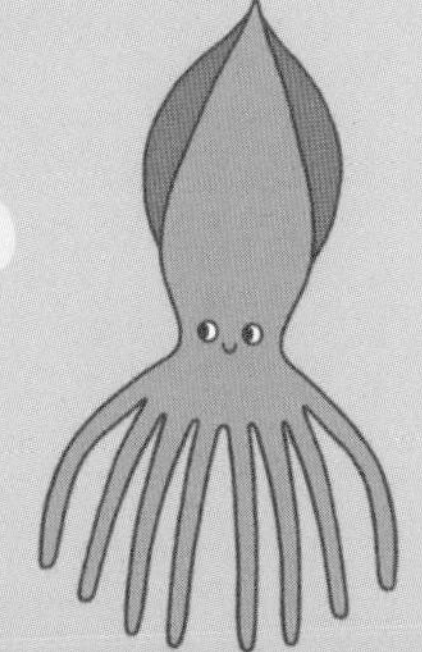

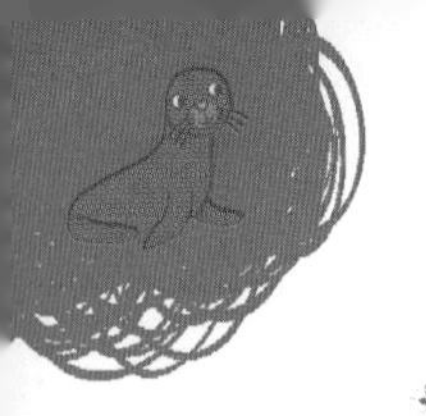

Can you draw a seal?

1 Start by drawing his round head.

2 Add his body. Don't forget to leave a gap at the bottom!

3 Draw his front flipper.

4 Add another front flipper and a back flipper. Give him a cute face, with a little pink nose!

Now it's your turn ...

Can you draw a sea snake?

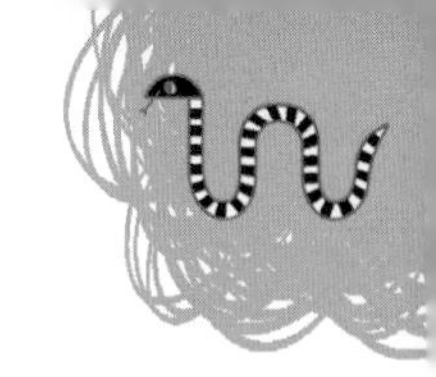

1 Start with half a circle for her head, and a long neck.

2 Add two "U" shapes to make her curvy body.

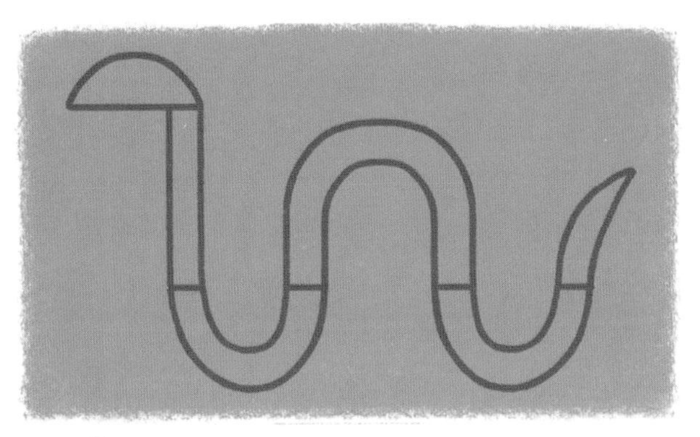

3 Add one more before finishing with her tail.

4 Give her an eye and a forked tongue, and add some bold, black and white stripes.

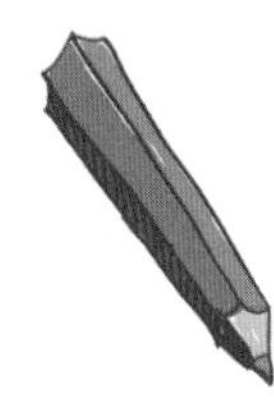

Now it's your turn.

Draw a yellow submarine.

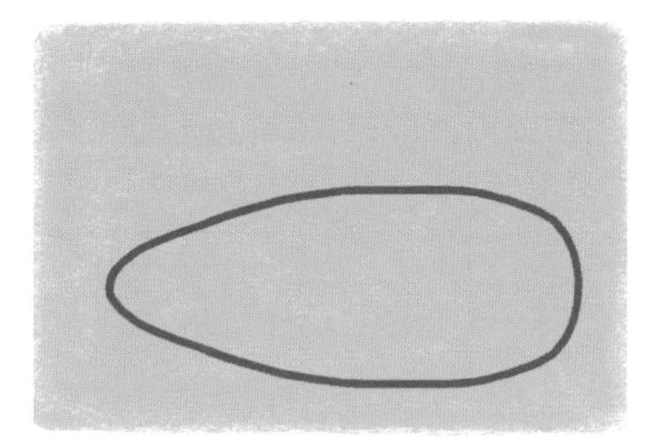

1 Start by drawing this shape for the submarine body.

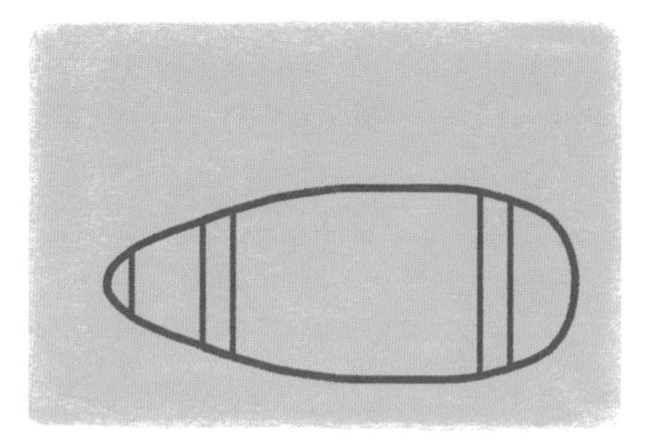

2 Draw some straight lines down the body like this.

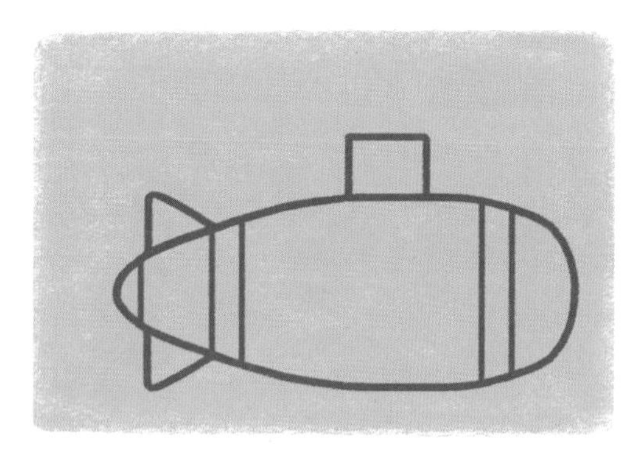

3 Add a square tower at the top and fins at the back.

4 Draw the rear propeller and some portholes. Don't forget the periscope!

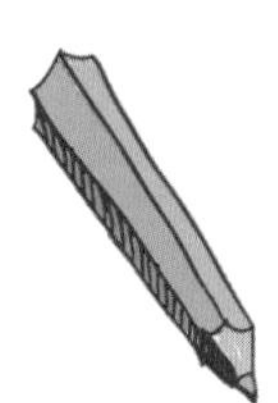

Now it's your turn!

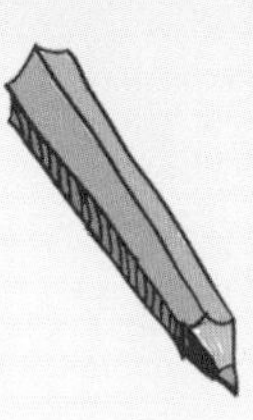

Draw a submarine deep under water.

Creepy-Crawlies

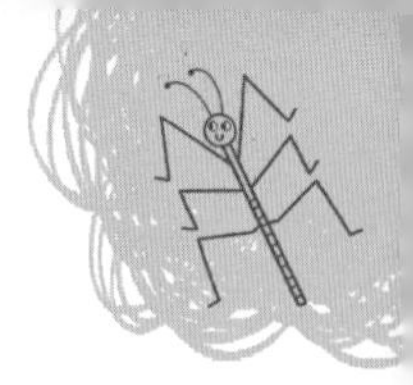

Let's draw a stick insect!

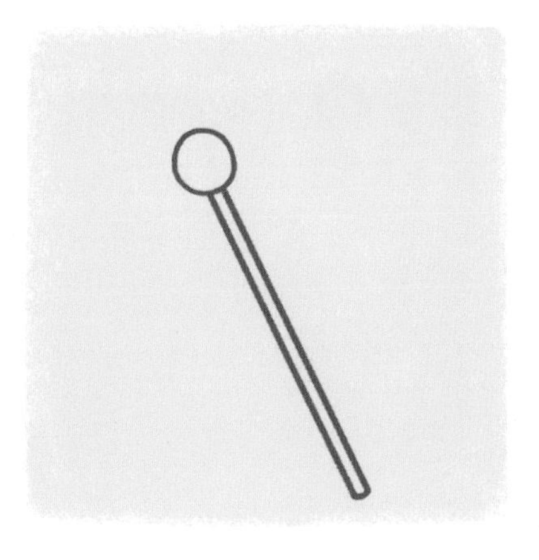

1 Start by drawing his round head and long body. It looks just like a stick!

2 Now add three thin legs on the left side of his body ...

3 ... and three thin legs on the right side!

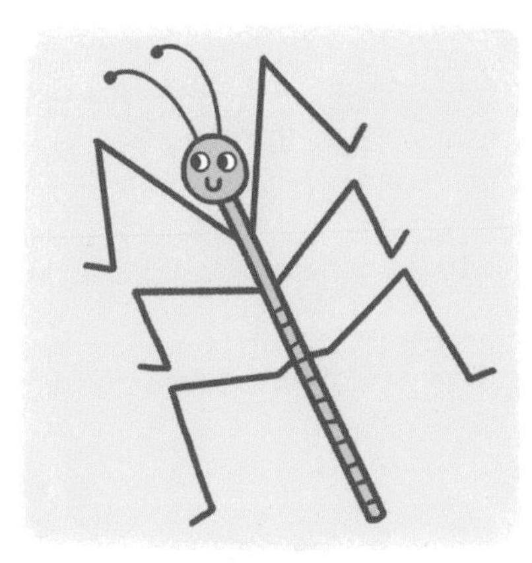

4 Give him some antennae and a nice smiley face. Make him green.

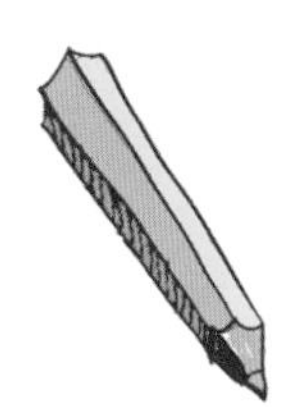

It's your turn now.

Draw a sweet spider!

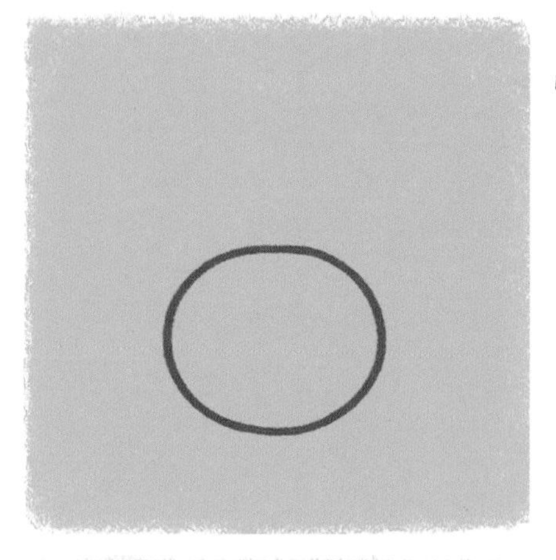

1 First draw a round shape for her head.

2 Now draw her body.

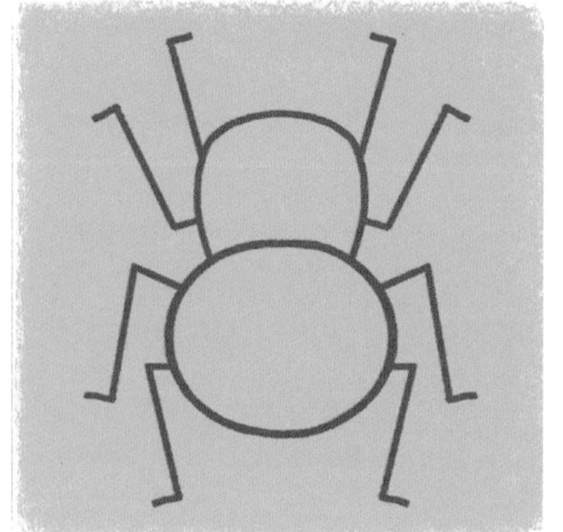

3 She has eight thin legs!

4 Add her face, and make her body black. She's not all that scary, is she?

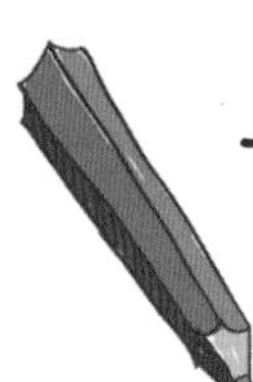

Try drawing a spider here.

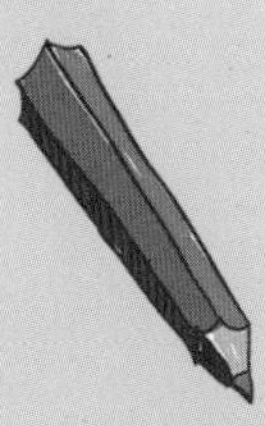

Draw a spider hanging from her web.

Draw a brilliant caterpillar.

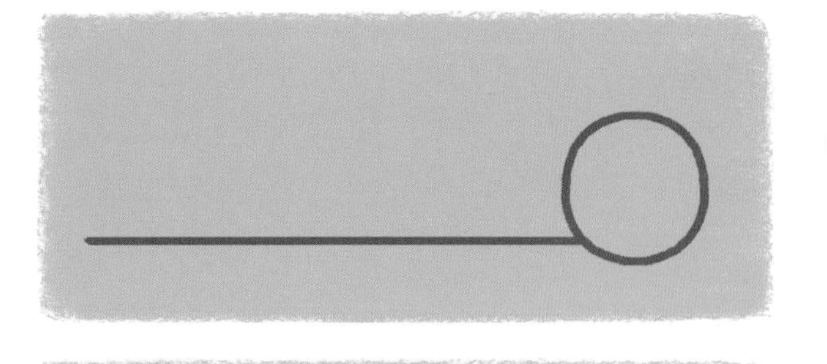

1 Start with the caterpillar's round head and a line for the base of his body.

2 Now add the sections of his body. There are five of them and they are round at the top.

3 Draw his little feet—one for each section of his body!

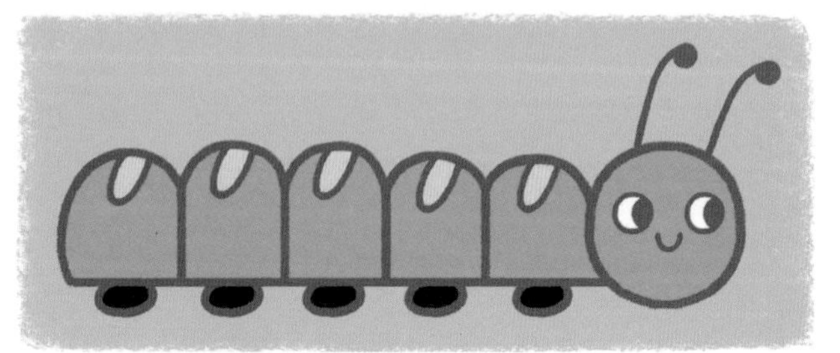

4 Draw his antennae and a friendly face. Make him a bright shade of green.

Draw your caterpillar here.

Can you draw a caterpillar on a leaf?
To turn a caterpillar into a millipede, draw lots of little legs!

What about a buzzy bee?

1 First draw the bee's round head.

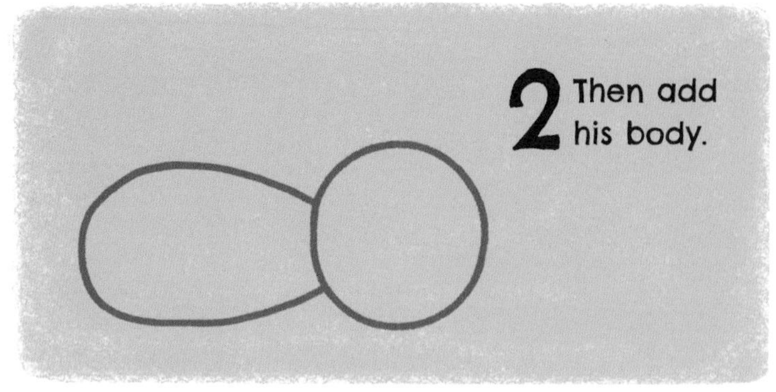

2 Then add his body.

3 Don't forget the stripes on his body and two wings.

4 Draw his antennae, face and six legs. He's yellow and stripy!

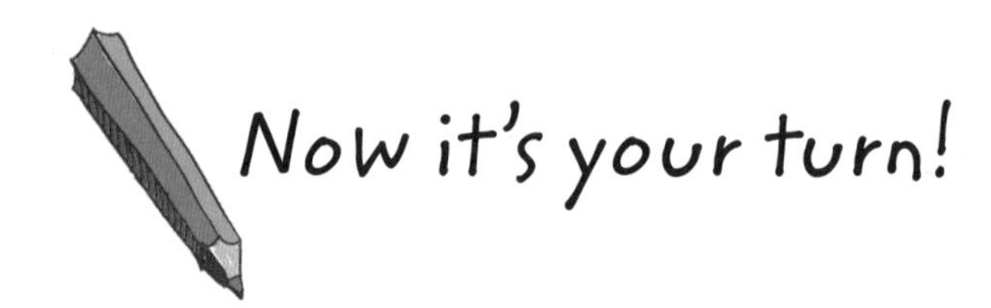

Or a dotty ladybug?

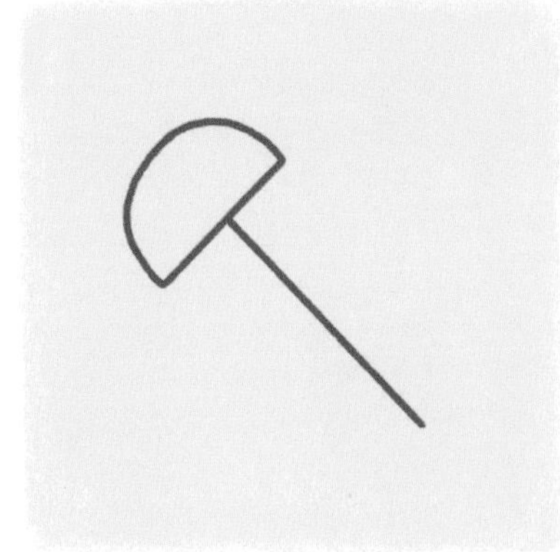

1 Start by drawing a semicircle for her head and a straight line for the middle of her body.

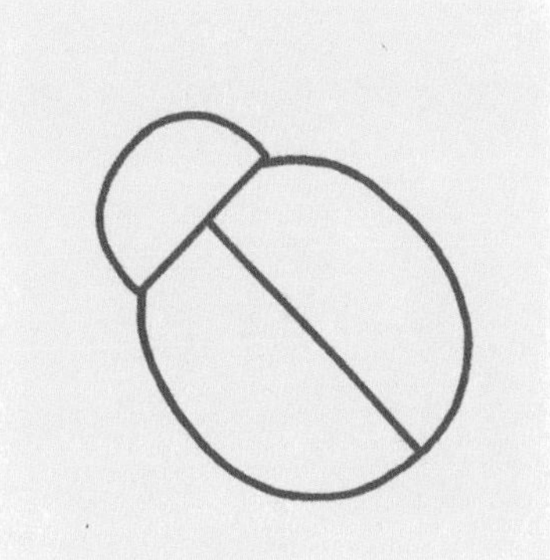

2 Now add a round shape to complete her body.

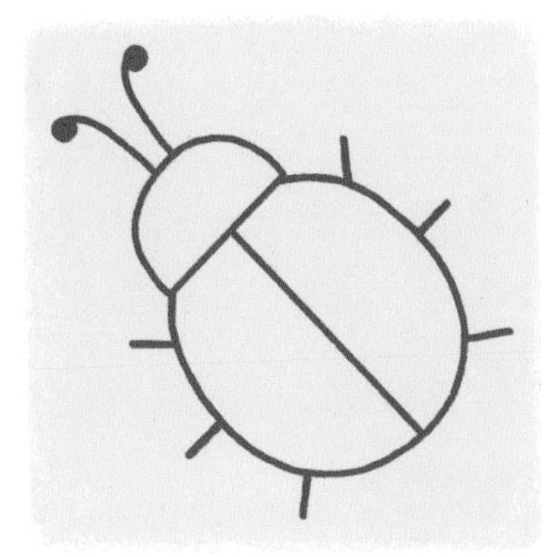

3 Draw her antennae and six little legs—three on each side.

4 Give her a cute face and lots of spots. Make her bright red with black spots.

Draw some ladybugs here.

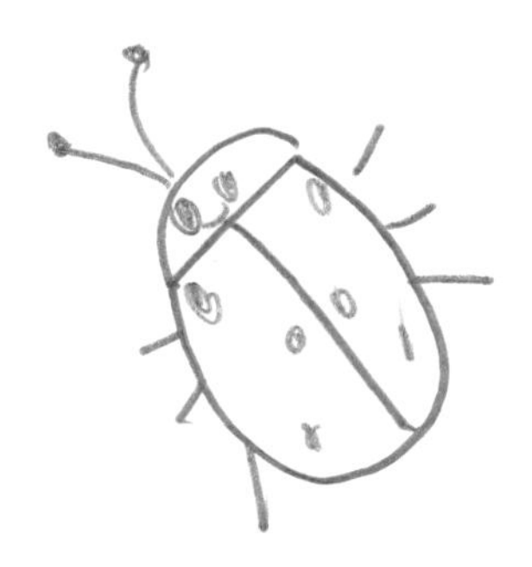

Can you draw a snail?

1 Begin by drawing a big, round shape for his shell.

2 Add his long body and round head.

3 Draw round and round to make the spiral.

4 Add his tentacles and happy face. Make him purple and orange.

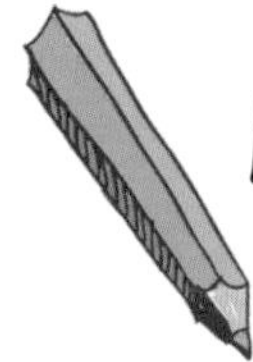

Draw a snail here!

Draw the snail that has eaten these leaves!

Try a beautiful butterfly!

1 First draw a circle for his head.

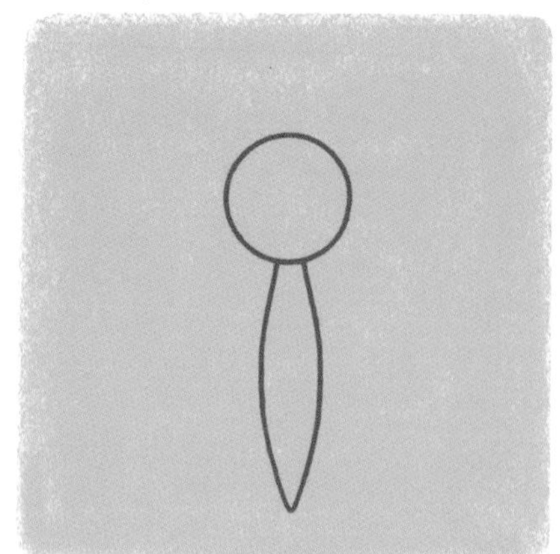

2 Now add his long, thin body.

3 He needs four curved shapes for his lovely wings!

4 Give him a happy face, and some antennae. Make patterns on his wings, and finish him in pretty shades of blue, yellow, or anything you like!

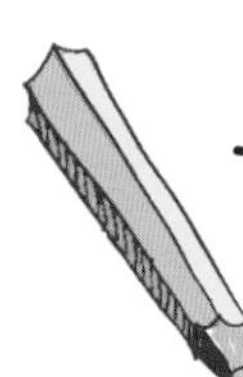

Try drawing a butterfly.

A butterfly starts life as a tiny egg. →

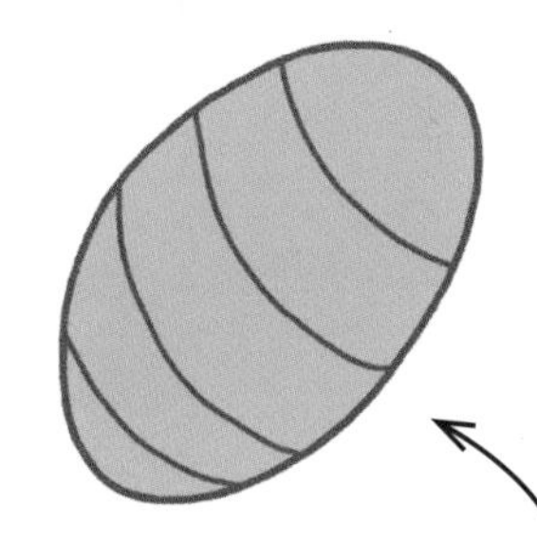

A wiggly caterpillar comes out of the egg.

The caterpillar then changes into a little case.

Later, a pretty butterfly comes out of the case.

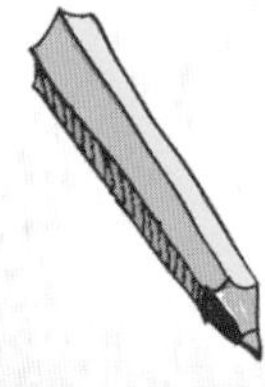

Can you draw all the stages of a butterfly?

Let's draw a grasshopper!

1 First, draw your grasshopper's head.

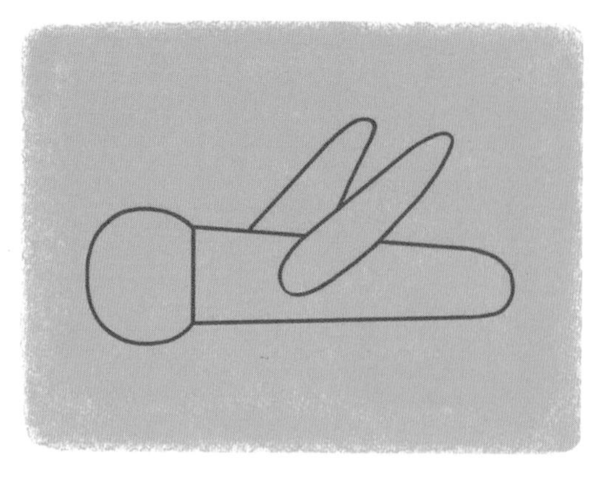

2 Now draw his long body and start his large back legs.

3 He has thin legs. His back legs are very long!

4 Draw his antennae and face, and make him green.

Draw a grasshopper here.

How about a beetle?

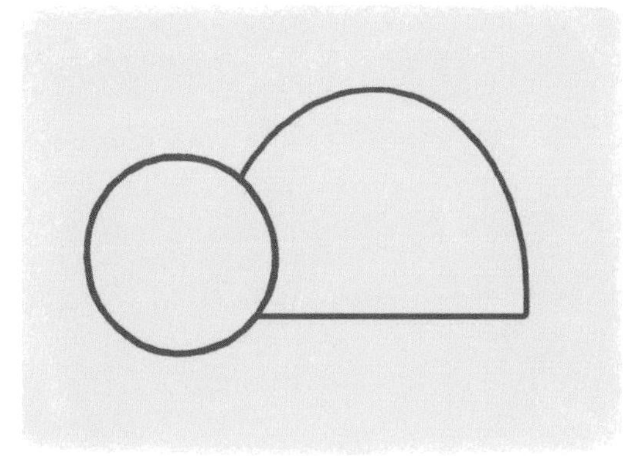

1 Start by drawing her round head.

2 Add a curved shape for her body.

3 She needs six tiny legs and some antennae.

4 Draw her face and a line for her wings. Finish her in shades of bright green.

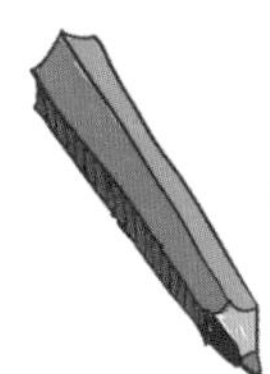

Now it's your turn ...

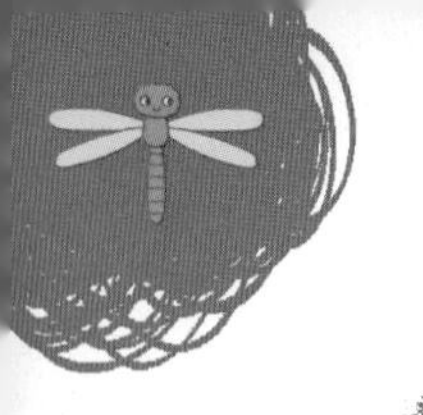

Try drawing a dragonfly.

1 Start by making her head a rounded shape.

2 Now draw the top part of her body.

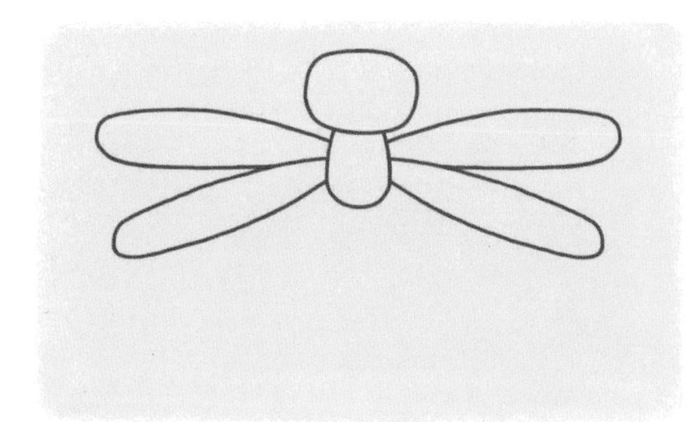

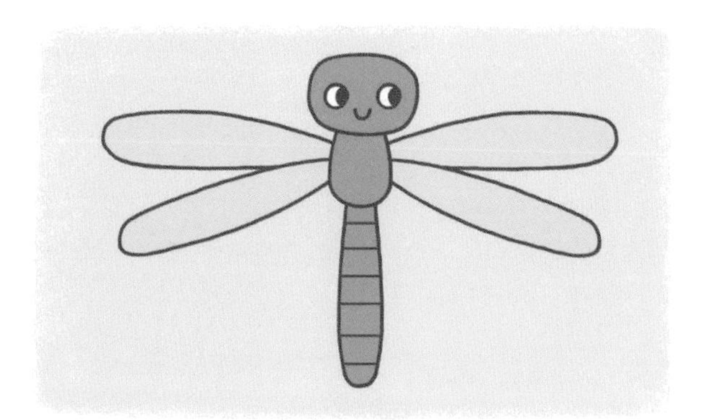

3 She has two pairs of wings.

4 Draw the bottom part of her body, and add her face. Give her pale-blue wings and a green body.

Draw your dragonfly here.

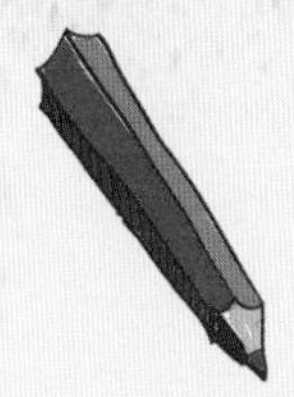

Give your dragonflies different-shaped wings ...

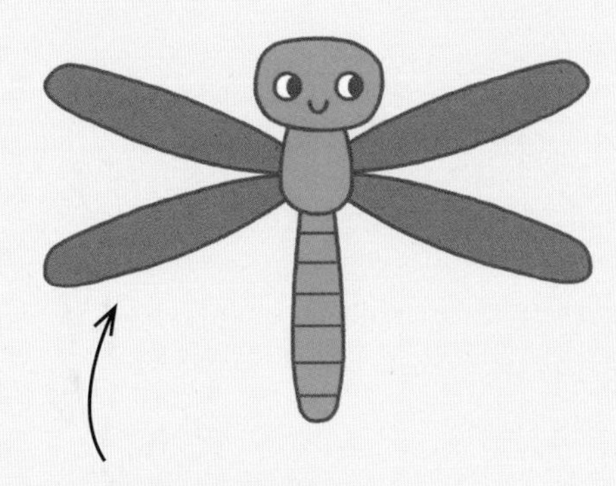

Try using bright purple for her wings.

Pastel shades look very pretty.

... and add a pond for them to fly over!

Shall we draw an ant?

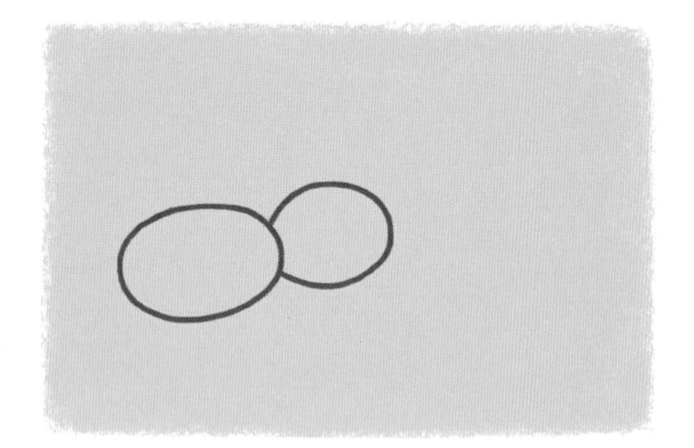

1 Draw a round head and the smaller part of his body.

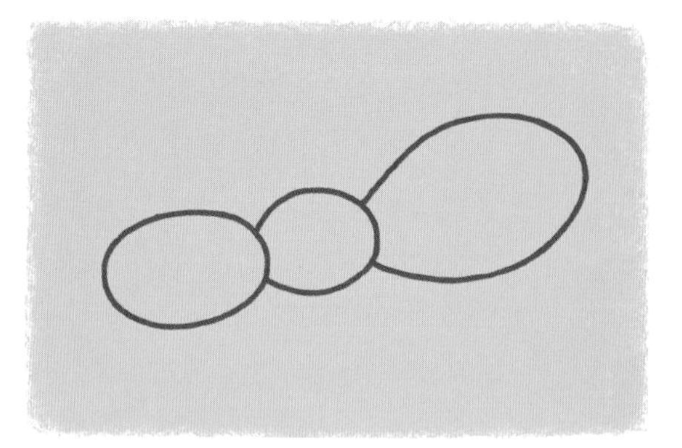

2 Now add the biggest part of the body.

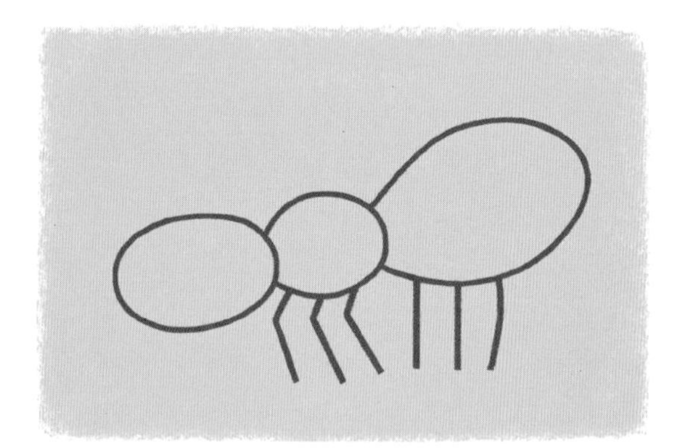

3 He needs six tiny legs.

4 Add his face and antennae, then finish him in brown, black, or red.

Can you draw an ant here?

Draw some ants scurrying around their anthill.

Things That Go

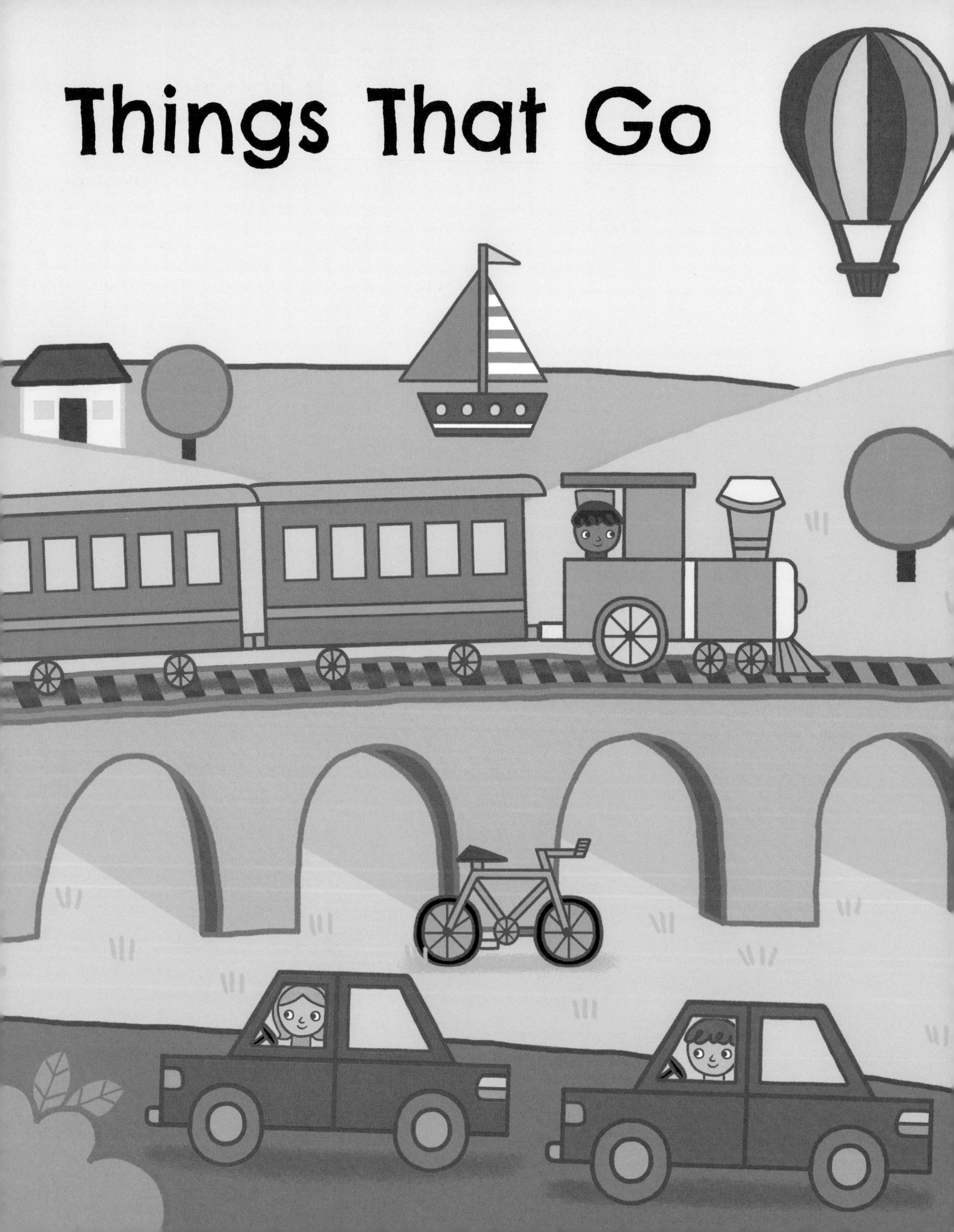

Can you draw a bicycle?

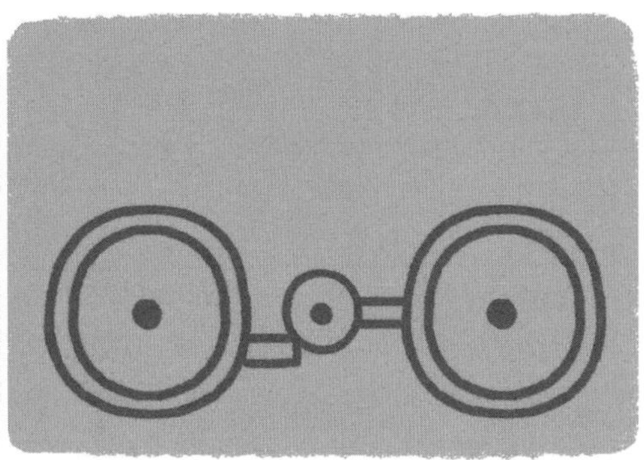

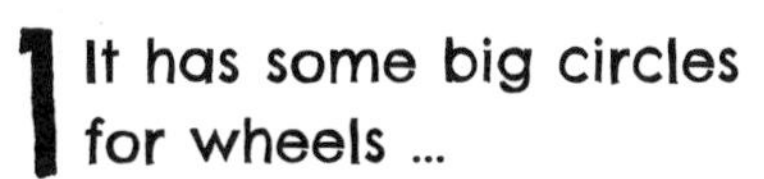

1 It has some big circles for wheels ...

2 ... and a little circle for the pedals.

3 Can you draw the frame?

4 Add the handlebars and seat and shade it in.

Now you have a try!

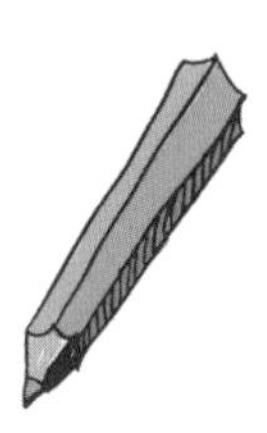

What about a train?

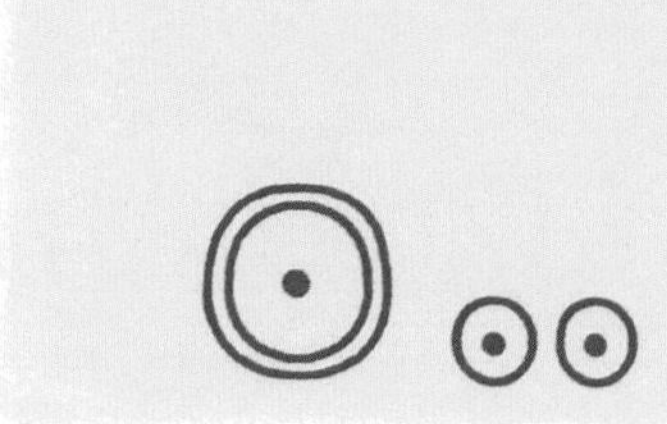

1 First, draw the wheels—one big and two small.

2 Add the main body of the engine.

3 Draw the cab where the driver will sit.

4 Don't forget details like the smokestack!

Can you draw a train across both pages?

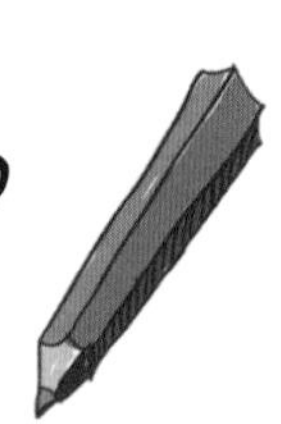

The train will need some carriages ...

1 Start by drawing a box shape.

2 Add some little wheels.

3 The carriage needs a roof ...

4 ... and windows. It's brightly painted!

Trains have different sorts of carriages.

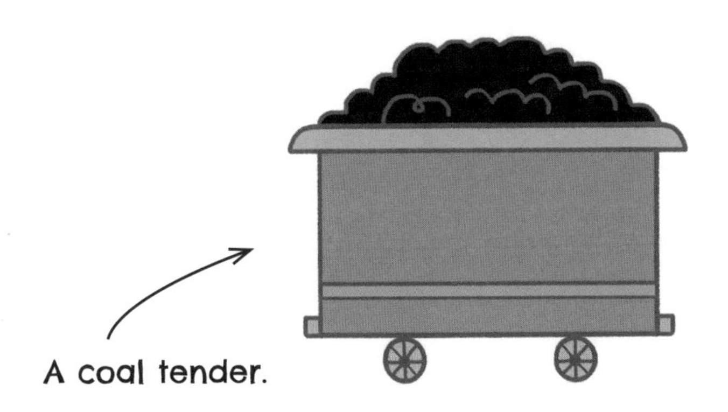

A coal tender.

A carriage for a circus train.

Choo-choo!

Draw a sailing boat ...

1 Draw this shape for the boat.

2 It needs a tall mast!

3 Add triangles for the sails.

4 Put a flag on top and add some portholes.

Now draw your own boats.

Let's draw a car!

Draw some cars here.

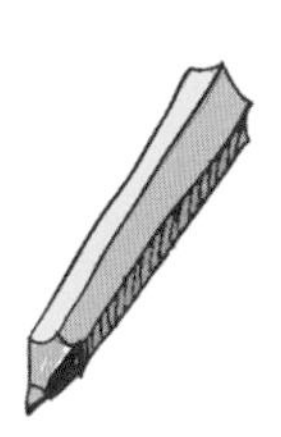

Try a speedy sports car.

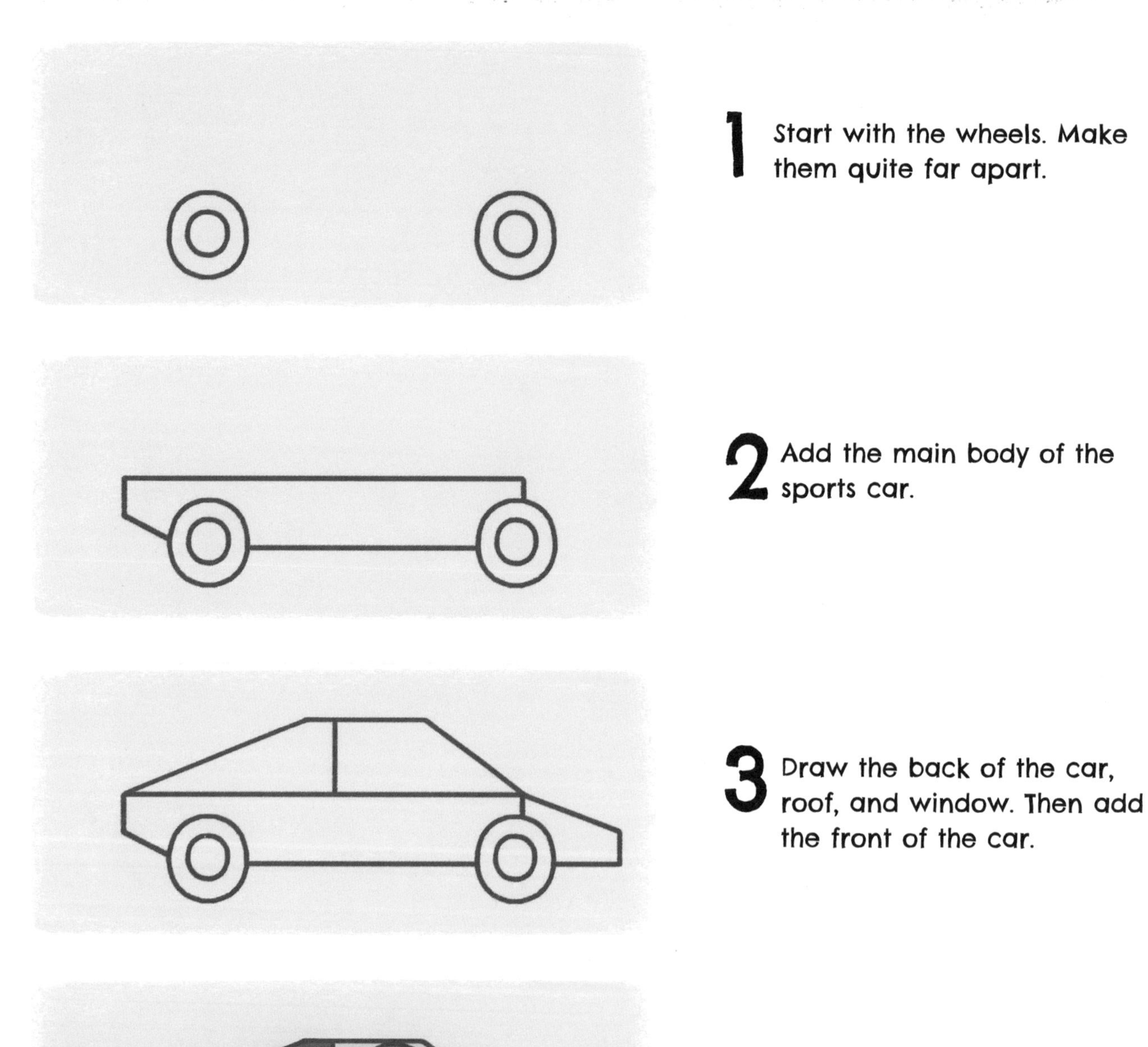

1 Start with the wheels. Make them quite far apart.

2 Add the main body of the sports car.

3 Draw the back of the car, roof, and window. Then add the front of the car.

4 Add details like the lights, steering wheel, and rear spoiler. Don't forget the driver!

What will your sports car look like?

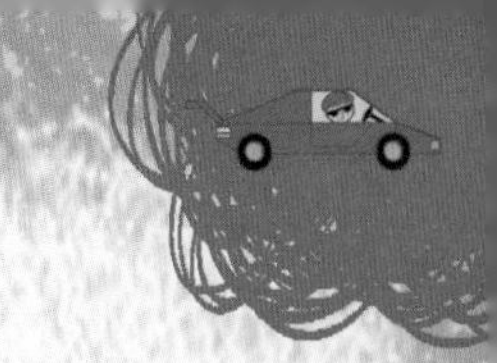

Draw your sports cars here ...

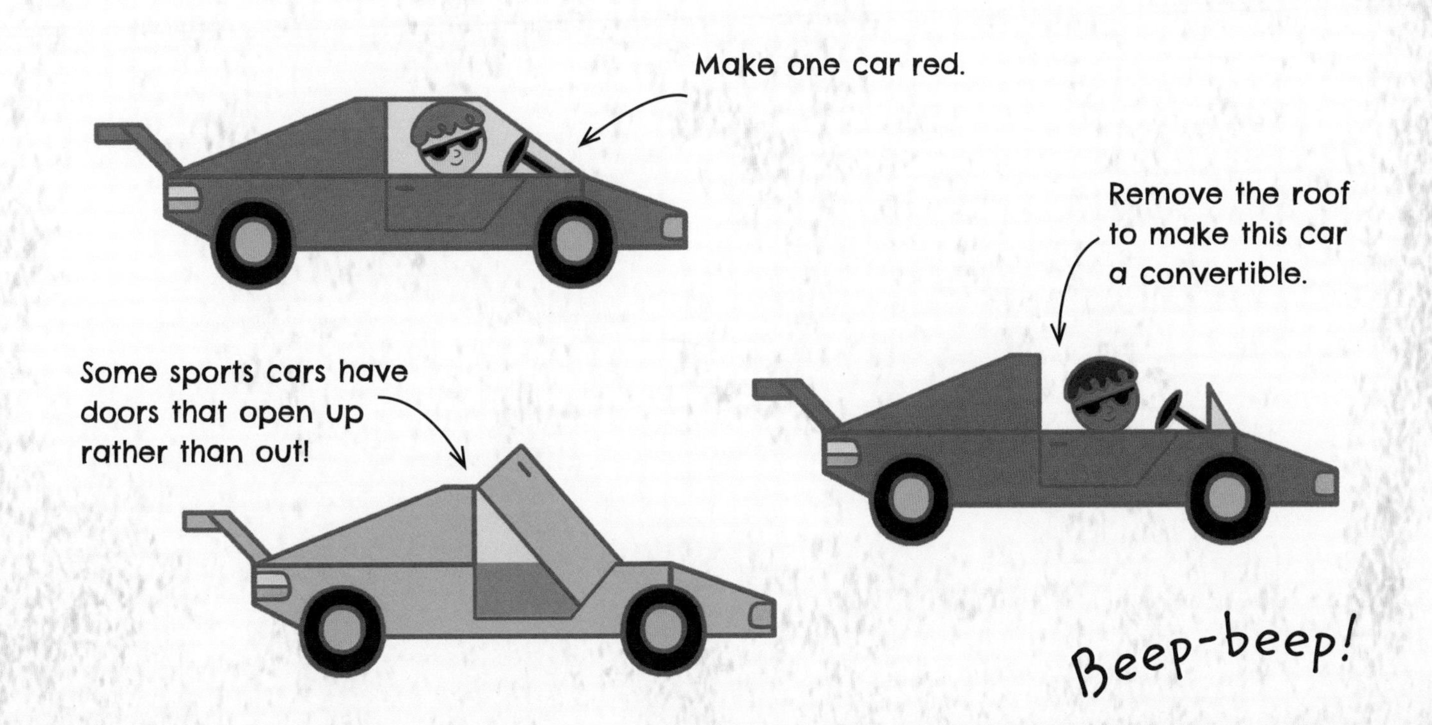

What about a motorcycle?

1 Start by drawing two wheels. The wheels are quite thin.

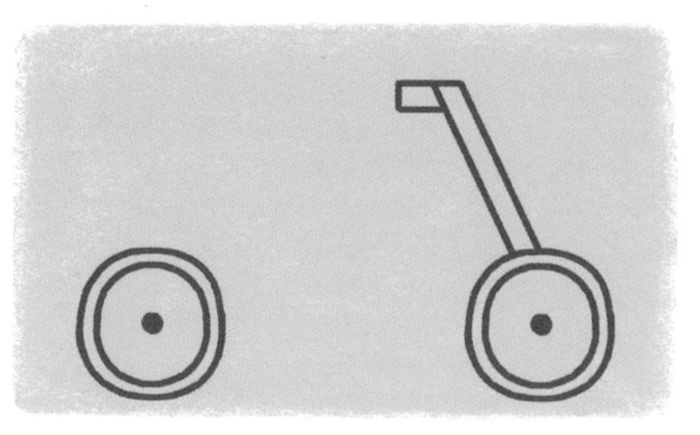

2 Add the front of the motorcycle and the handlebars.

3 Now add the main body of the motorcycle.

4 Draw a comfy seat and some lights. Don't forget the footrest.

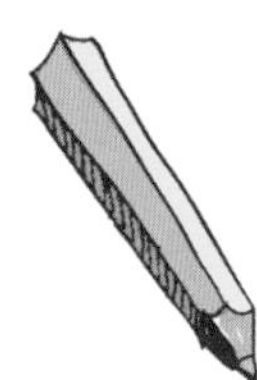

Can you draw one as well?

Why not draw the rider?

Can you fill the road with motorcycles?
This motorcycle has a sidecar for a passenger!

Let's try a hot-air balloon.

1 Begin with a simple circle.

2 Draw in the ropes ...

3 ... and a basket for the passengers.

4 Hot-air balloons are brightly patterned!

Can you draw one here?

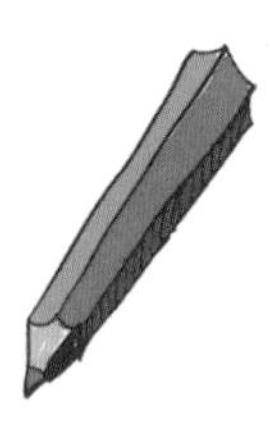

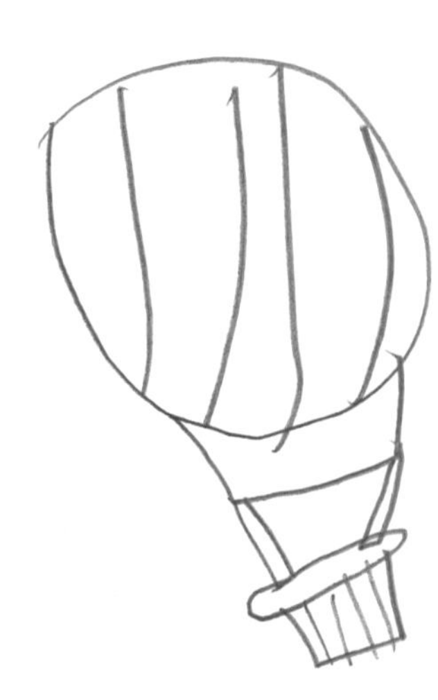

Draw some balloons in the sky.

Let's draw a jet plane.

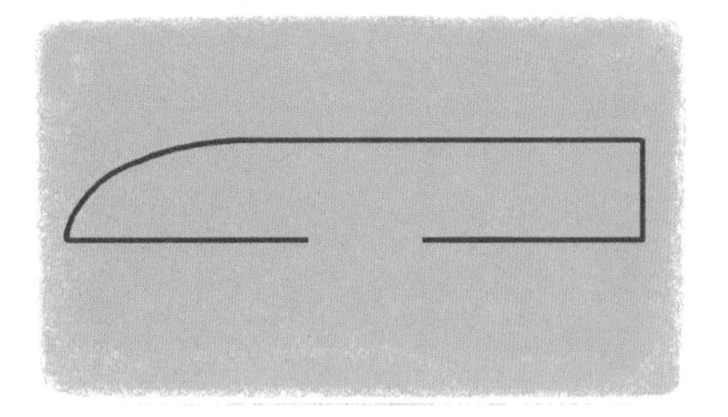

1 Draw a long shape for the body of the plane. Leave a gap at the bottom.

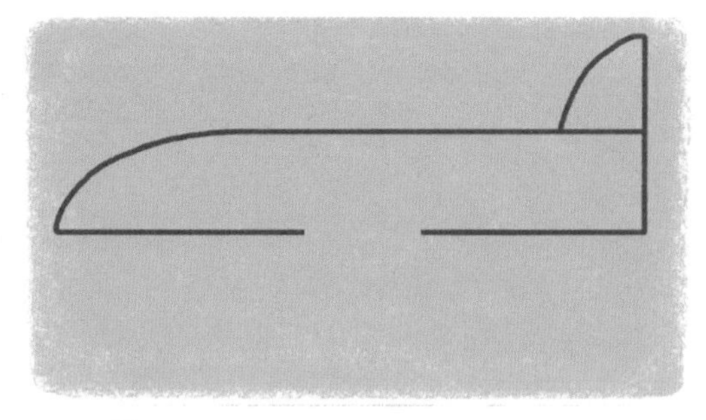

2 Don't forget to add a tail fin ...

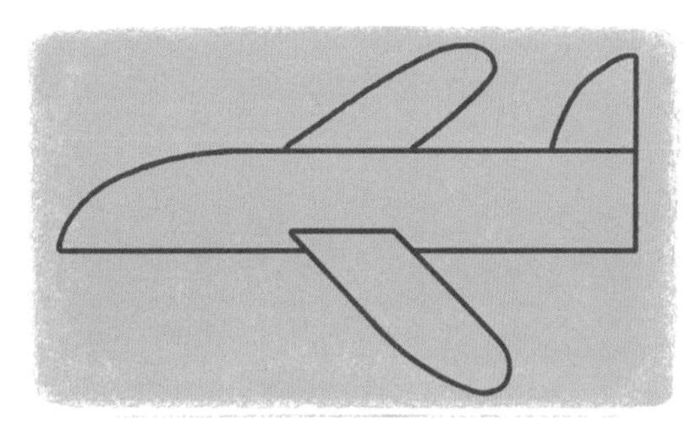

3 ... and two wings!

4 Draw the windows and use blue to fill them in.

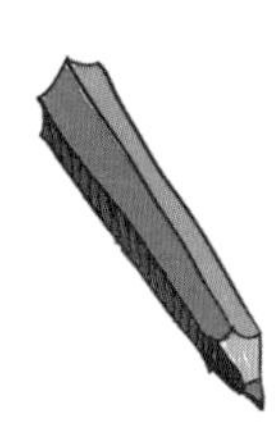

Try drawing your own plane.

Mind the birdie!

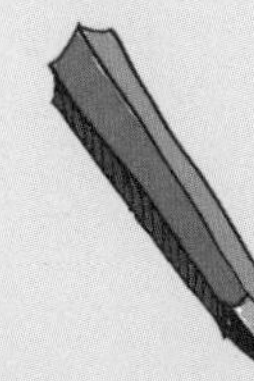

How many jet planes can you draw in the sky?

What about a seaplane?

1 Start with the body of the seaplane. Leave a gap at the bottom.

2 Add a wing and the front strut.

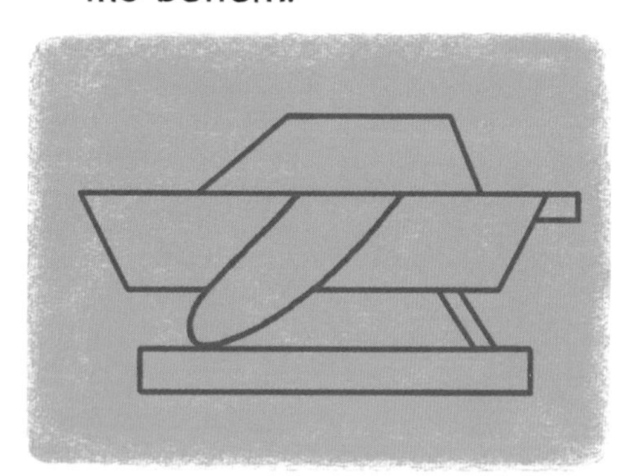

3 Now draw the cabin and the float under the plane.

4 Add some windows, the tail fin and propeller, then do the paintwork.

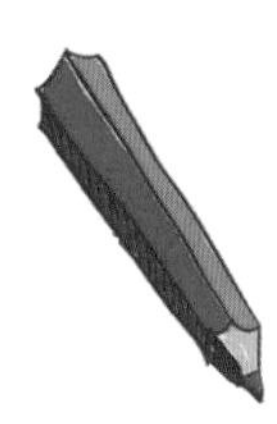

Draw a seaplane here.

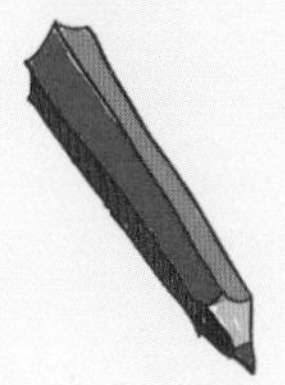

Can you draw a seaplane in the sky ...

... and one that has landed on the water?

Now try a hovercraft!

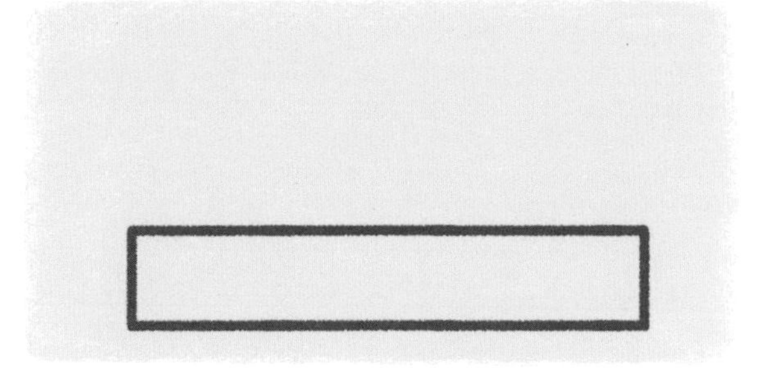

1 To begin, draw a long rectangle.

2 Add curved ends. This is the base of the hovercraft.

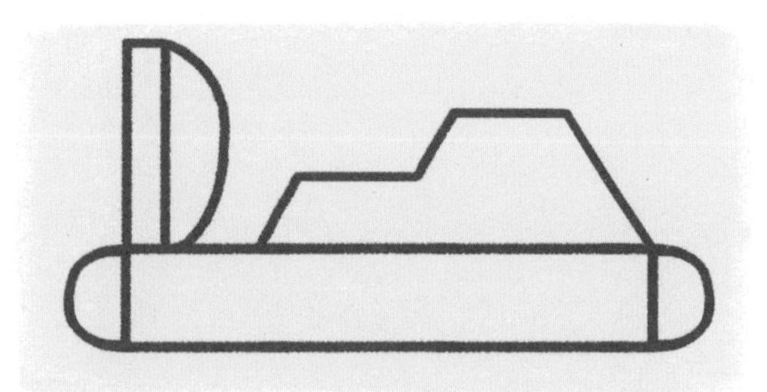

3 Now draw the cabin and the big fan at the back.

4 Add some windows and the radar at the back, Give it an orange cabin and fan.

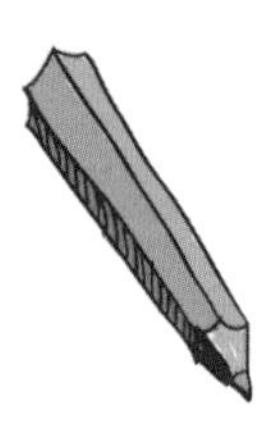

Try drawing a hovercraft here.

Draw a hovercraft racing a speedboat!

Now let's try a fire truck.

1 Begin with the base and two wheels.

2 Draw the cab at the front and a line at the back.

3 Add the light on the top and some windows. Draw the sides of the ladder.

4 Finish the ladder and add some lights. Then add the store for the fire hose.

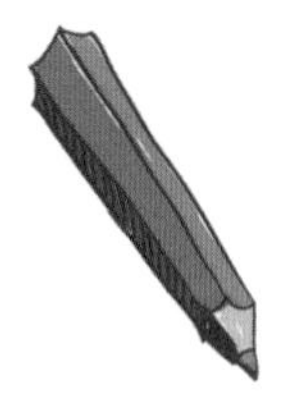

Draw your own fire truck here.

Can you add a firefighter driving the truck?

Draw a fire truck helping to put out a fire.

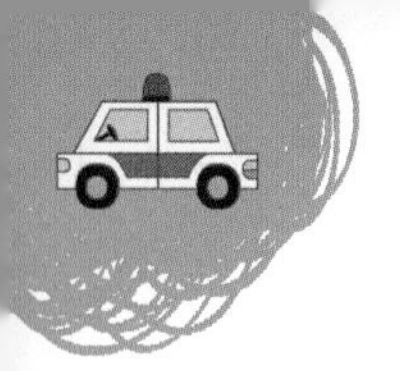

What about a police car?

1 Start by drawing two wheels.

2 Draw two rectangles for the body of the car.

3 Add the roof of the car with the flashing light on top.

4 Draw some windows and a steering wheel, and add some lights front and back.

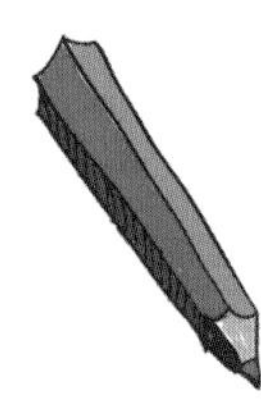

Can you draw a police car?

Draw some police cars chasing
the robber in his getaway car!

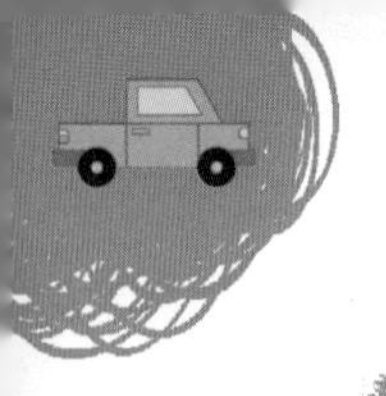

Draw a pickup truck.

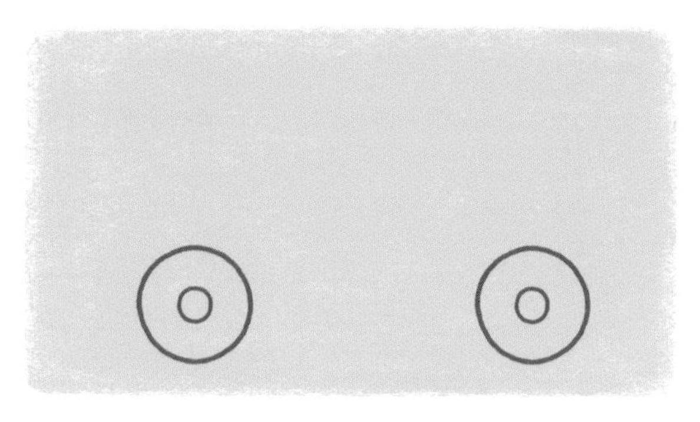

1 Begin by drawing two wheels.

2 Add some straight lines like these to form the body.

3 Draw the bumpers and the cab of the truck.

4 Finish by adding a window, a door handle and some lights.

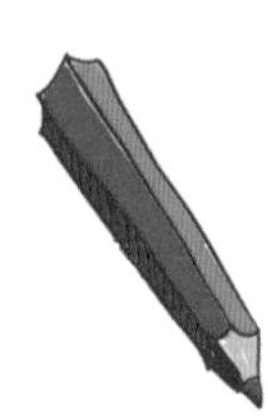

Draw a pickup truck here.

Who is driving your truck?

Can you draw a snowplow?

Start by following steps 1 and 2 for the truck.

3 Draw the bumpers and cab. Then add a snowplow blade at the front.

4 Finish with a window and some tail-lights, and draw a flashing light on top.

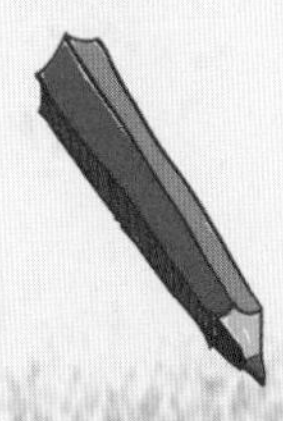

Draw a pickup truck and snowplow here.

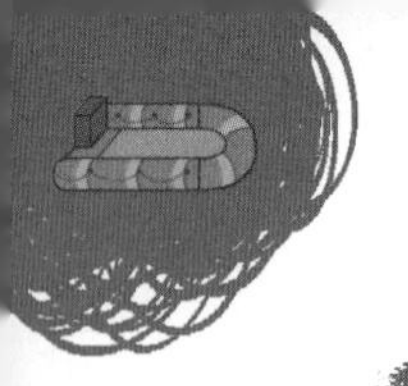

Can you draw a lifeboat ...

1 Begin with a box shape like this.

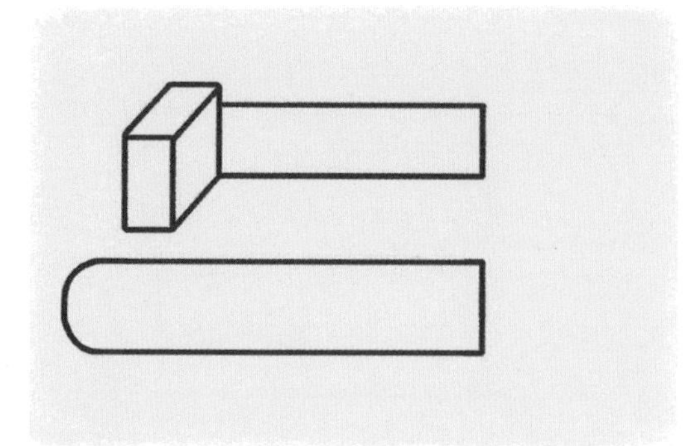

2 Draw two more shapes to form the sides of the boat.

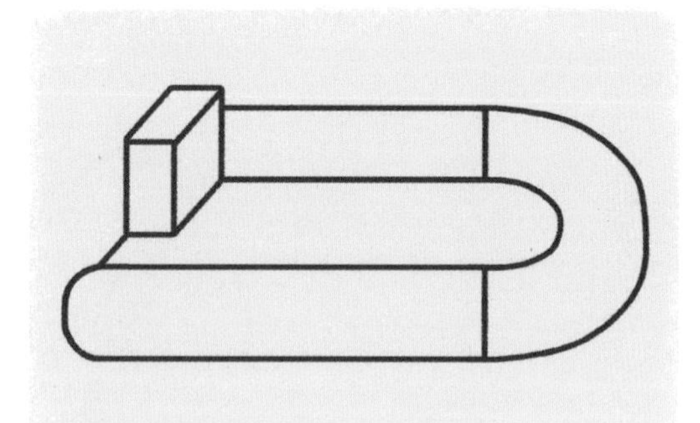

3 Add a rounded shape for the front of the boat and finish the back.

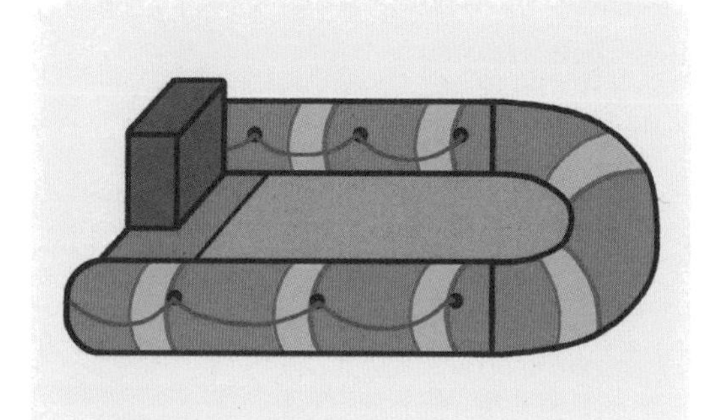

4 Draw stripes around the sides, add a rope to each side, and give it stripes.

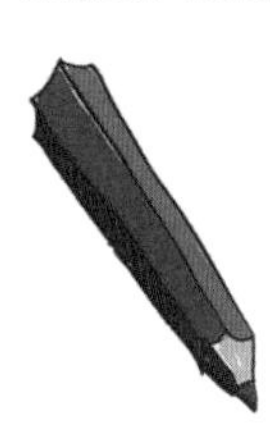

Draw your lifeboat here.

... or a rescue helicopter?

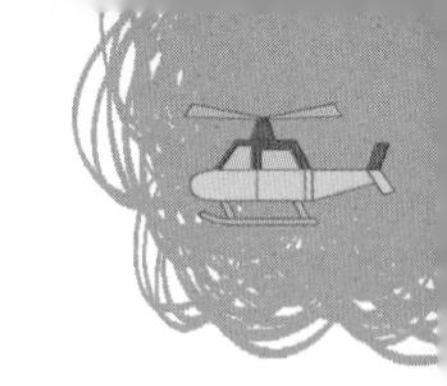

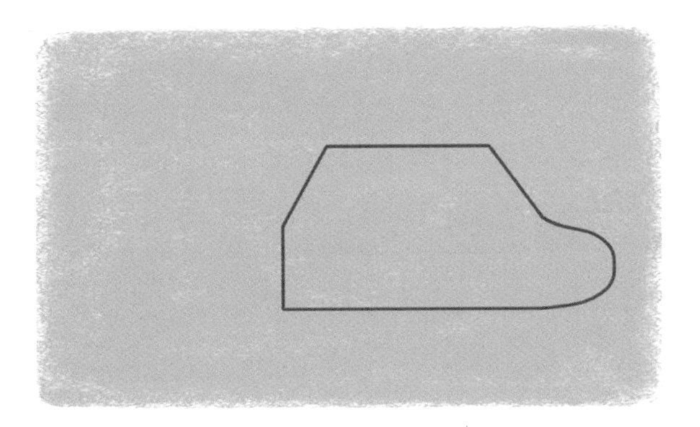

1 Start your helicopter by drawing this shape for the cockpit.

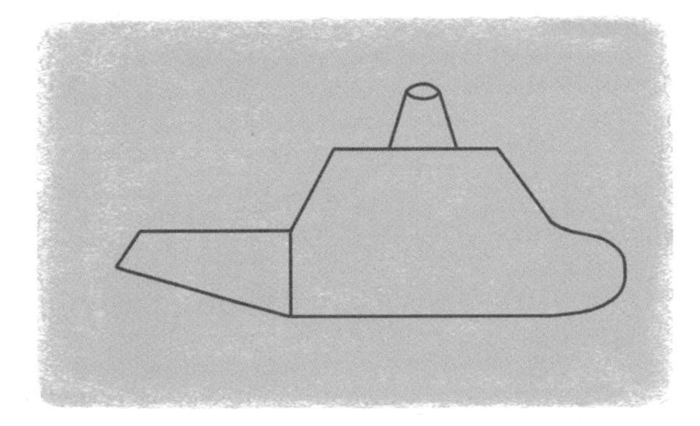

2 Add the tail of the helicopter and a cone shape on the top.

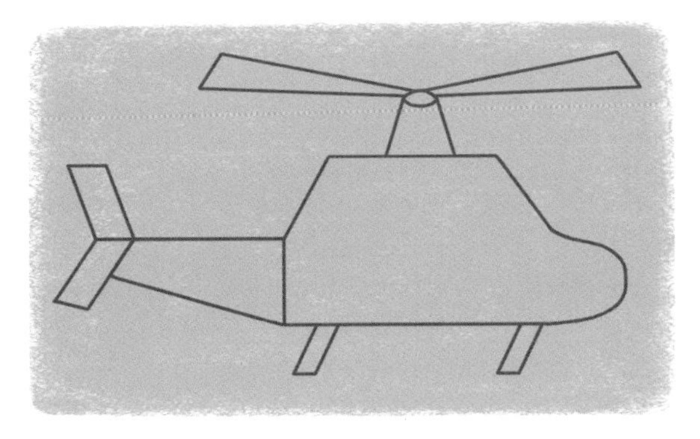

3 Draw the rotor blades at the top, the fins at the back, and two struts at the bottom.

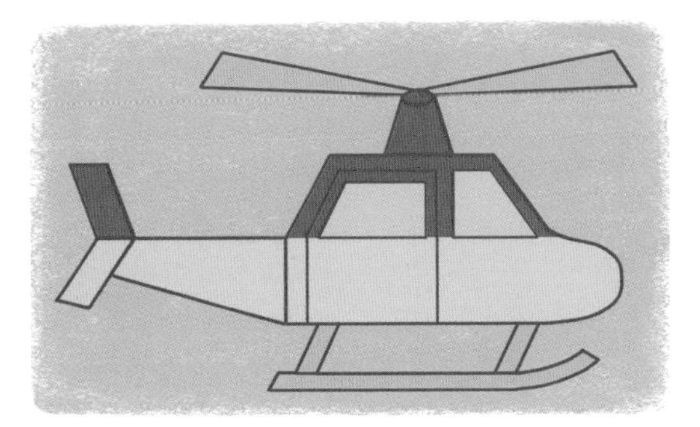

4 Finish by adding a door, windows, and the landing skid. This one's red and yellow!

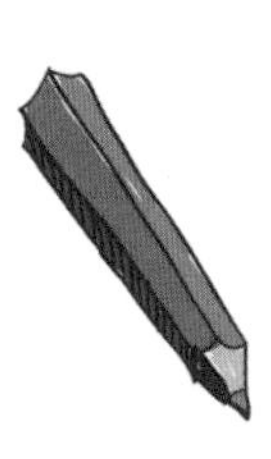

Draw a helicopter here!

Let's draw a moon buggy.

1 Start by drawing two wheels.

2 Now add the base and the wheel arches.

3 The astronaut needs a seat and control panel.

4 Pick out the different parts of the buggy in red, white, and black. Don't forget to add the satellite dish!

Try drawing a moon buggy here.

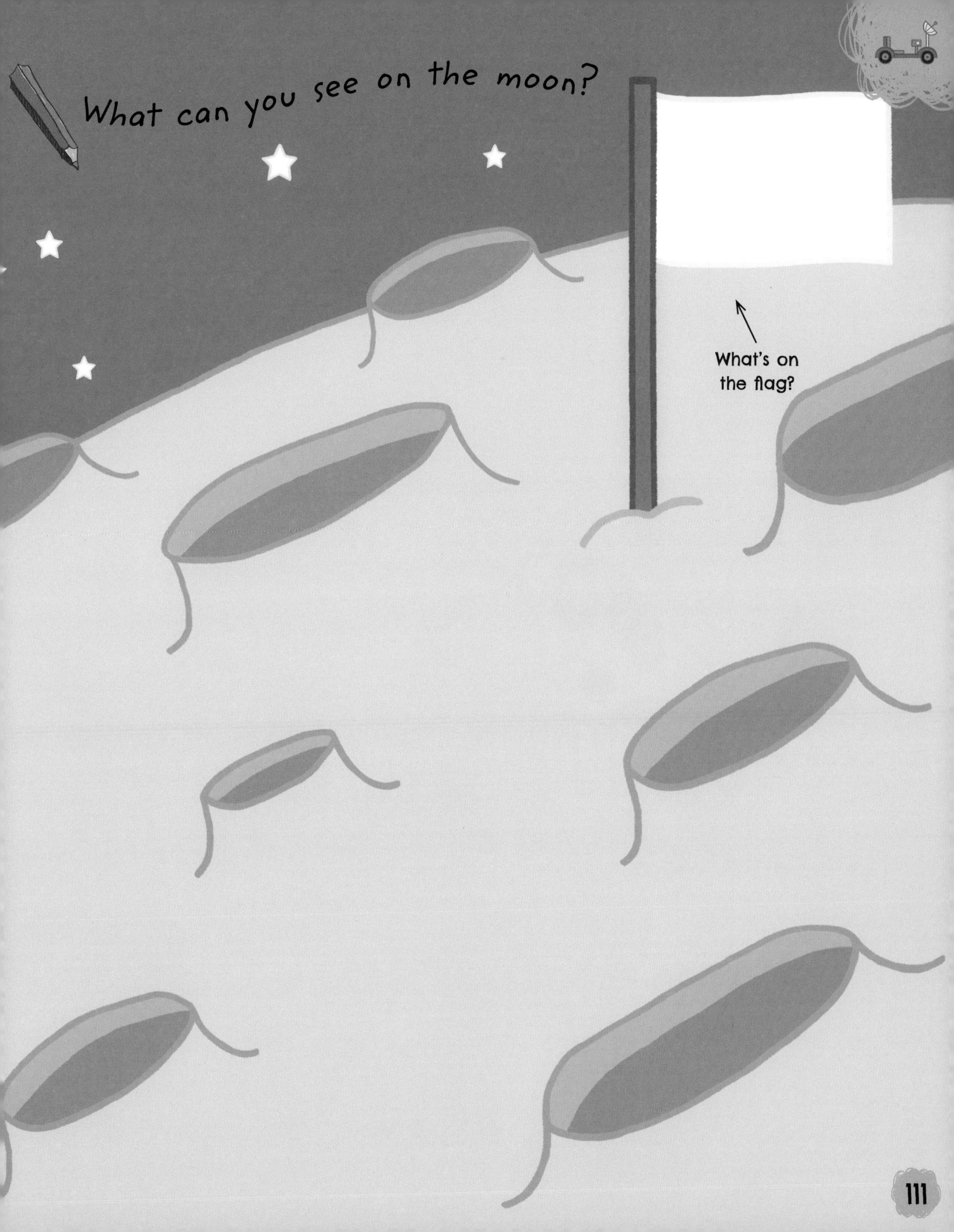
What can you see on the moon?
What's on the flag?

Pets

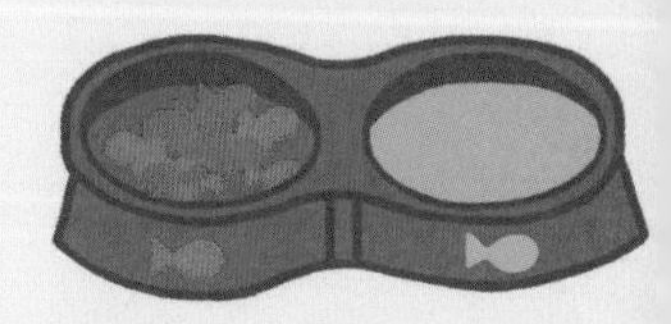

Draw a bunny rabbit!

1 Draw her head and long ears.

2 Now give her a body and one leg.

3 Add shapes for the rest of her legs.

4 She has a cute face and a fluffy white tail!

Try drawing a rabbit here.

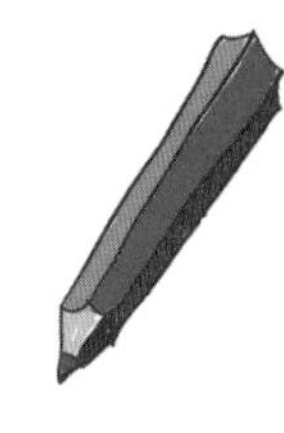

Let's draw a cute cat!

1 First, draw his head and ears.

2 Now draw in his body.

3 He needs legs and a long, curly tail.

4 Add his face, and give him a pretty pattern!

Draw your kitty here!

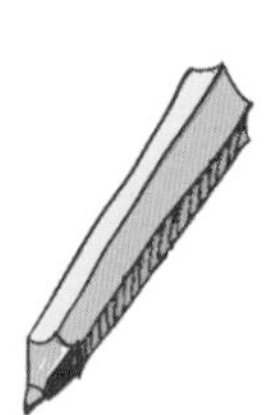

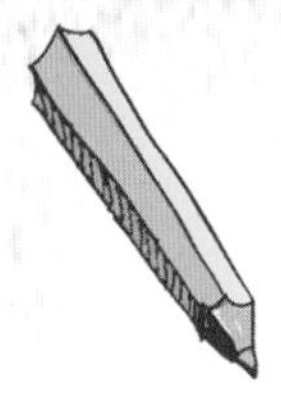

Can you draw a cat sitting down?

1 Start with his head again.

2 His body looks a bit different.

3 Add his front legs and tail.

4 There, he's finished!

This cat is black and white.

This tabby cat has a toy mouse.

This cat has a ball of wool.

You can draw lots of different cats!

Draw a playful puppy.

1 Start with the puppy's head and floppy ear.

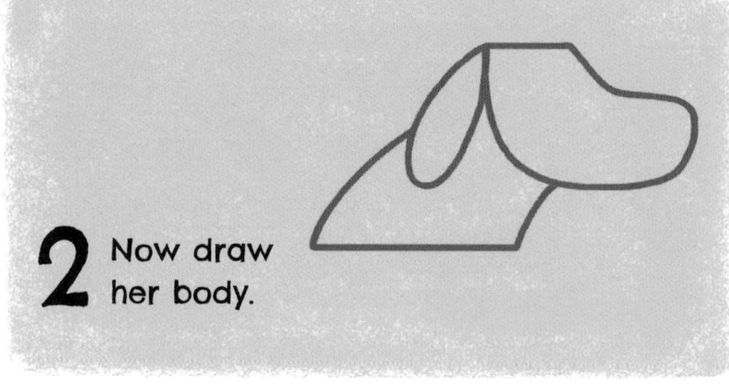

2 Now draw her body.

3 She needs four legs.

4 Draw her face and tail. Give her a pink nose!

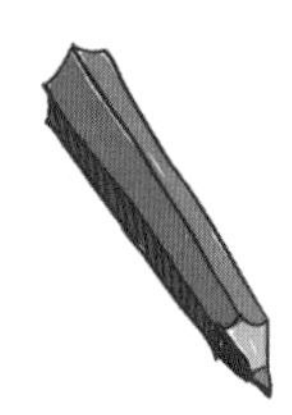

Now you can try!

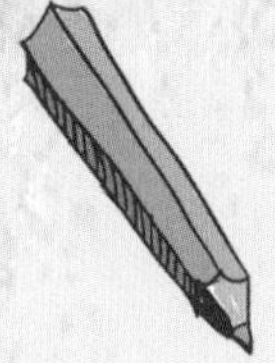

What kind of dog is Emily taking for a walk?

Can you draw more dogs in the park?

What about a tortoise?

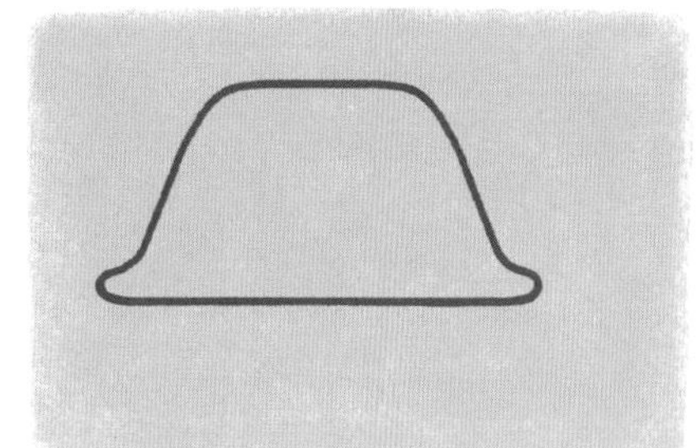

1 Let's start with his shell.

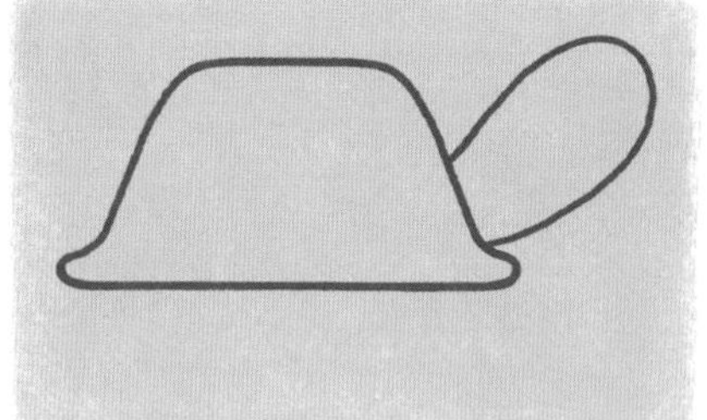

2 He has a long neck.

3 Draw his little stumpy legs.

4 Make him any shade you like!

Now you try.

Draw some tortoises in the garden.

Learn to draw a goldfish!

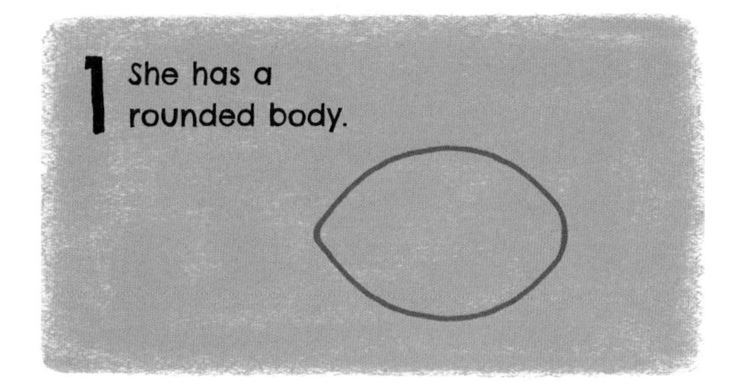

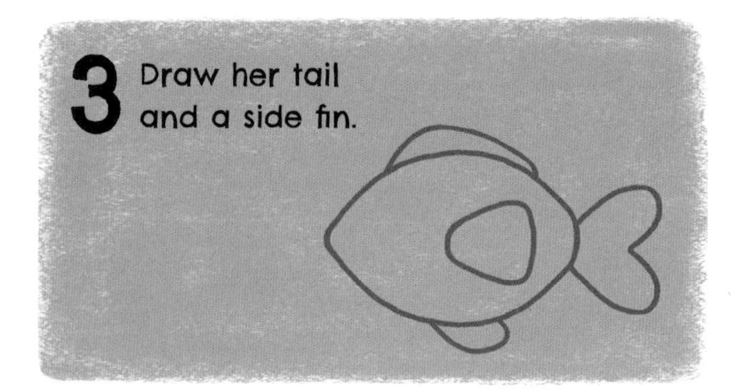

Try drawing a goldfish here!

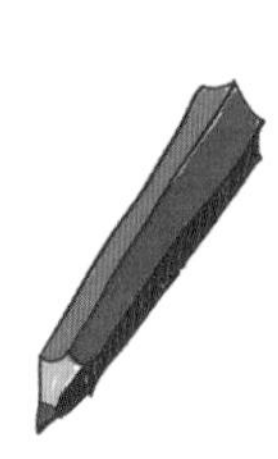

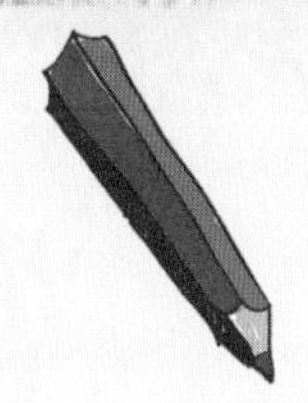

Draw some goldfish in the fish bowl!

Let's draw a hamster.

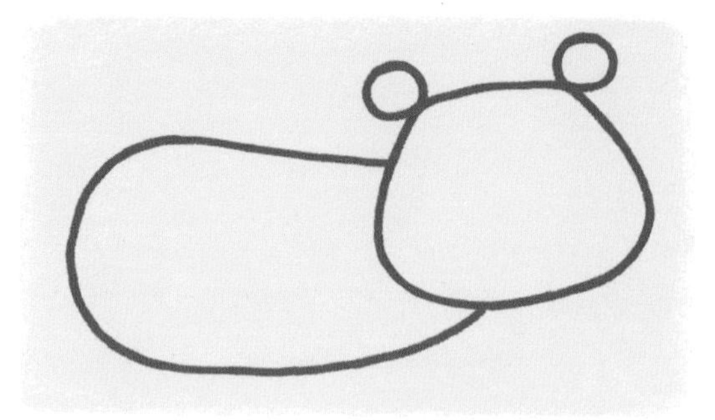

1 Start with his head and little ears.

2 Add his rounded body.

3 He has little legs and a stumpy tail.

4 Draw his face and make sure he has a fluffy coat!

Try drawing a hamster here.

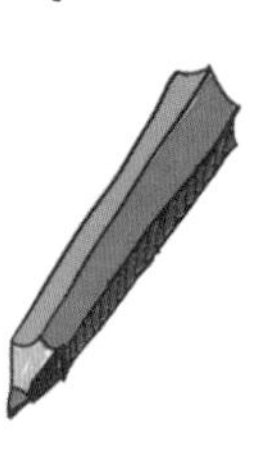

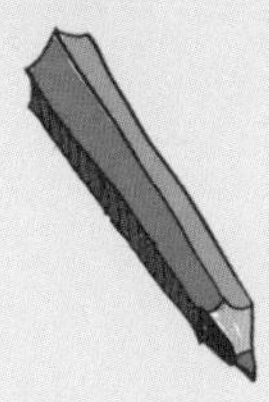

Can you draw a hamster in his wheel?

Draw a parakeet.

1 Here is her feathery head.

2 Now she has a feathery wing.

3 Add her legs and a long tail!

4 Draw her face and feet. Isn't she pretty?

Now try drawing some parakeets.

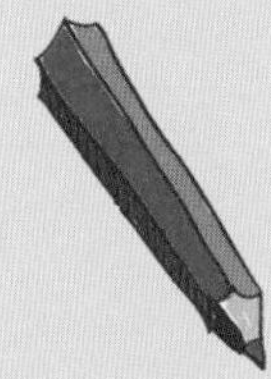

Draw different pets eating their food.

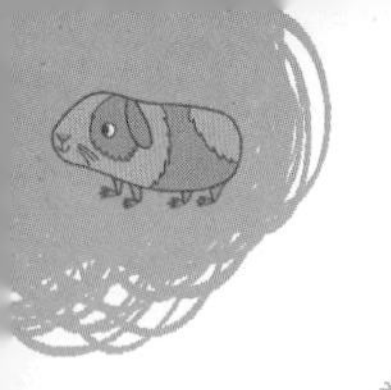

Draw a guinea pig ...

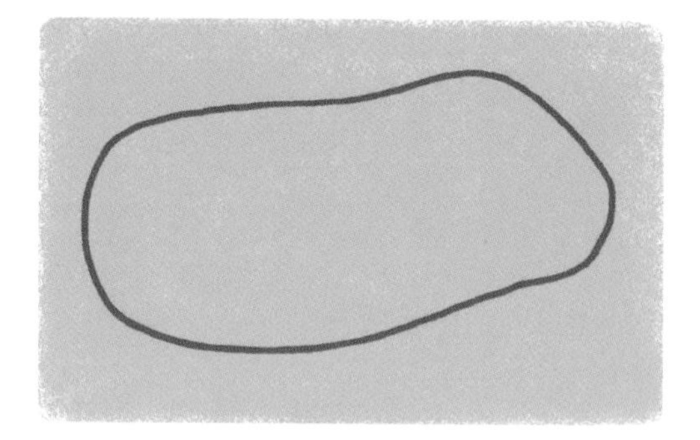

1 Draw this shape for her head and body.

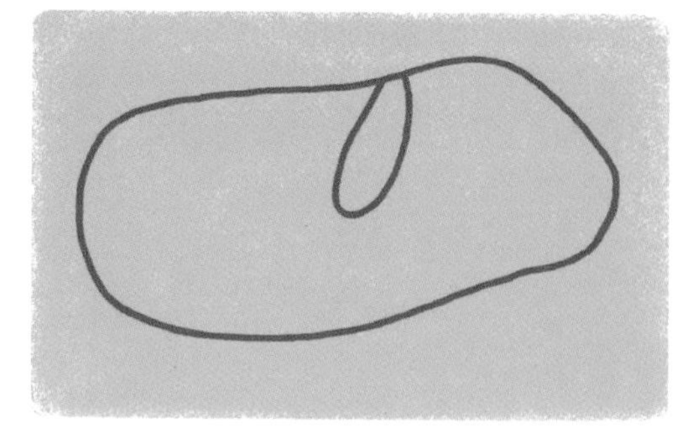

2 Now add her cute floppy ear.

3 She has four little legs and tiny feet.

4 Draw her face and shade her soft fur.

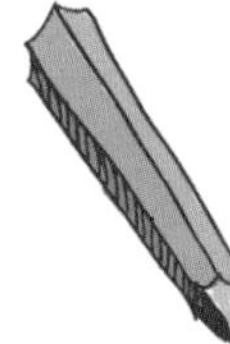

Can you draw a guinea pig here?

... or a scampering mouse!

1 He has two round ears and a pointed nose.

2 Now add his body.

3 Draw his legs so that he is running. Don't forget his long tail!

4 Draw his face, feet, and whiskers. Add dots of pink for his ears and nose.

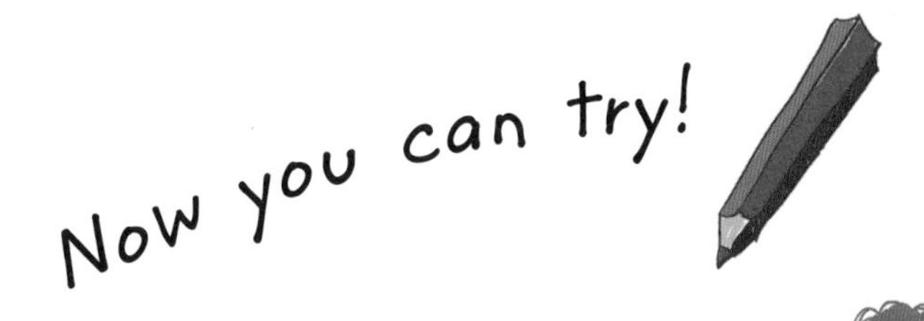

How about a horse?

1 Start with a rectangular shape for her body.

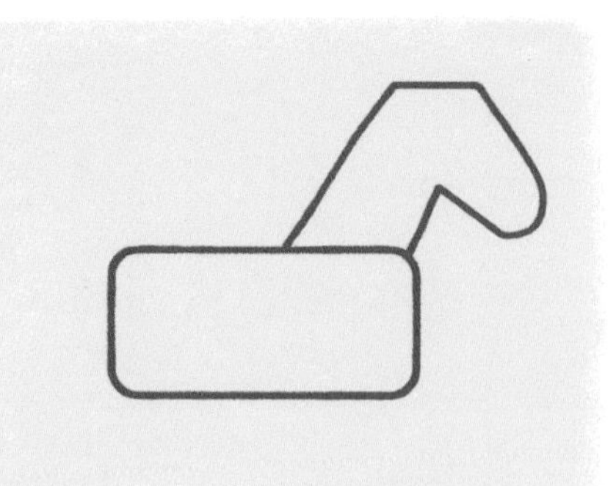

2 Draw this shape for her head.

3 Now add her four long legs.

4 She has a wavy mane and tail. Draw her face and ears, and shade her in.

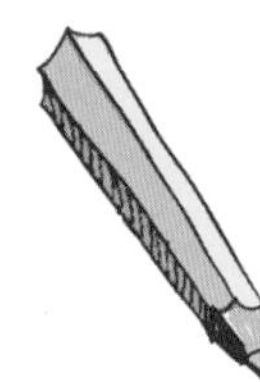

Try drawing a horse here!

Draw some horses in the field.

What are they doing?

Dinosaurs

Let's try a Tyrannosaurus rex!

1 Start with her head and body.

2 She needs a mouth, a tail and feet.

3 Don't miss her little arms, sharp teeth, and spines!

4 Add the final details and shade her in. Does she look very fierce?

Draw your own your Tyrannosaurus rex here!

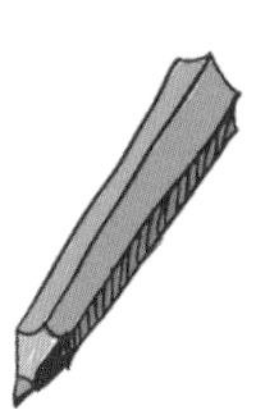

Now let's try a Triceratops.

1 Begin with this shape for her head.

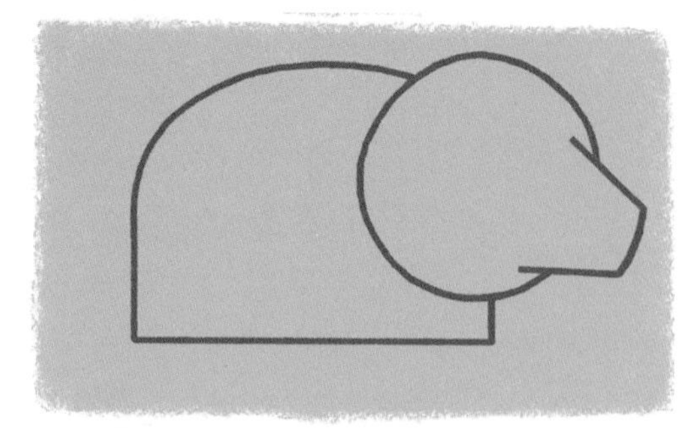

2 Add her body. She's quite big, isn't she?

3 Draw her tail and her little stumpy legs.

4 Add her face, and don't forget she has three horns!

Now you draw a Triceratops.

Can you draw the Triceratops that made these footprints?

Now draw a Diplodocus!

1 First, draw this shape for his body.

2 Then add four strong legs.

3 He has a little head, a long neck and a huge tail.

4 Draw his face and make him green. We gave him purple spots. too!

Draw a Diplodocus eating from the tree.

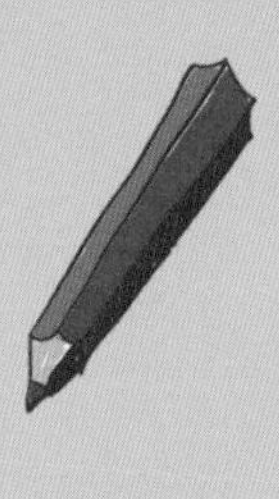

What about a Spinosaurus?

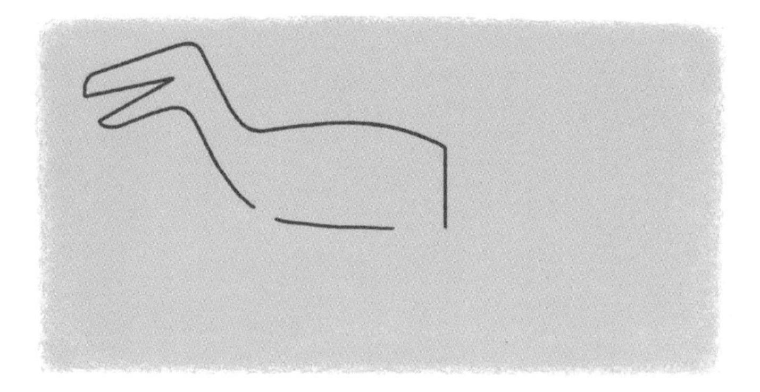

1 Start by drawing the head and body of your Spinosaurus (SPINE-oh-SORE-us).

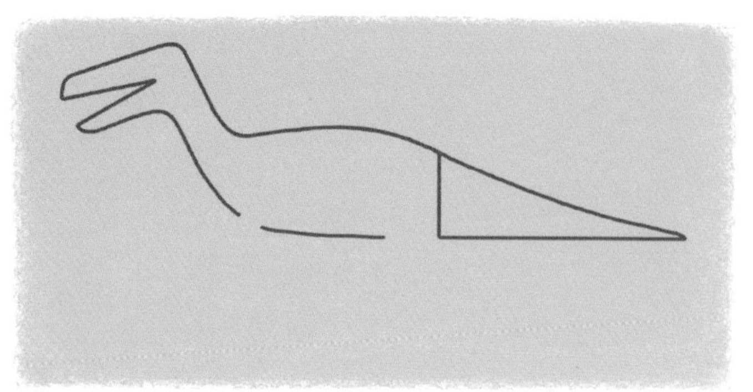

2 Add her long, pointed tail.

3 Give your Spinosaurus long legs and a curved sail on her back.

4 Finish by adding her face and short front legs. Give her sharp claws.

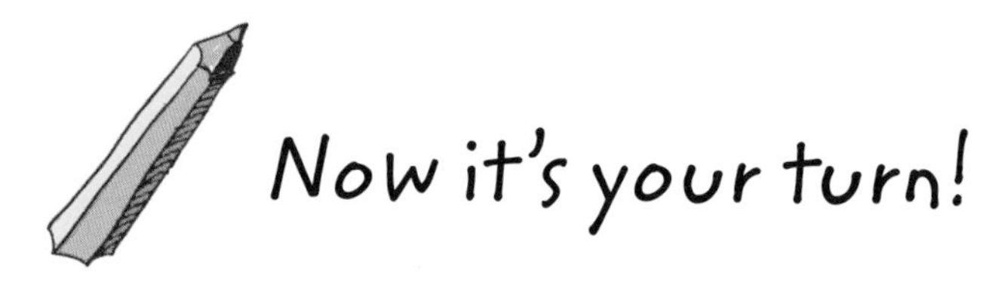

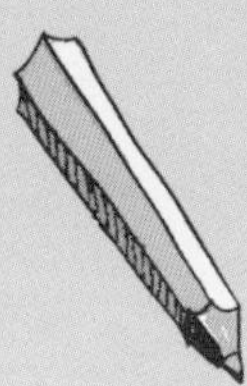

Try drawing a Spinosaurus on the riverbank.

Learn to draw an Anzu.

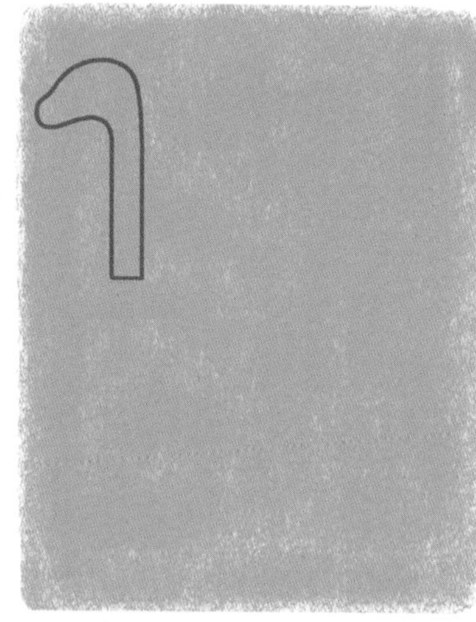

1 First draw the head and long neck for your Anzu (AN-zoo).

2 Draw this shape for his body and leg. Don't forget to leave a gap for his wing!

3 He needs a crest on his head, a pointed tail, and a feathery arm.

4 Finish off his feet and wing claws, draw his face, and give his some tail feathers.

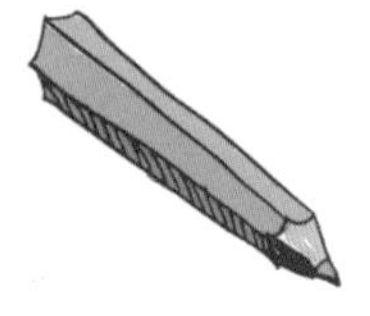

Try drawing an Anzu here. ⟶

Draw some Anzus fleeing from the volcano!

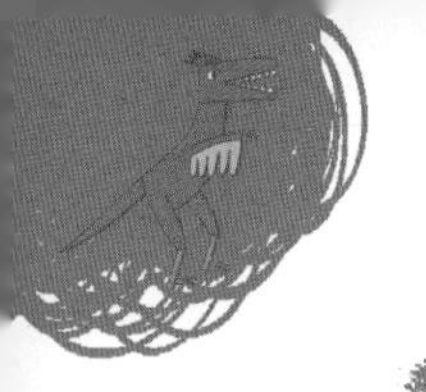

Can you draw a Troodon?

1 Begin by drawing the head for your Troodon (TROH-oh-don). Give him a big, open mouth.

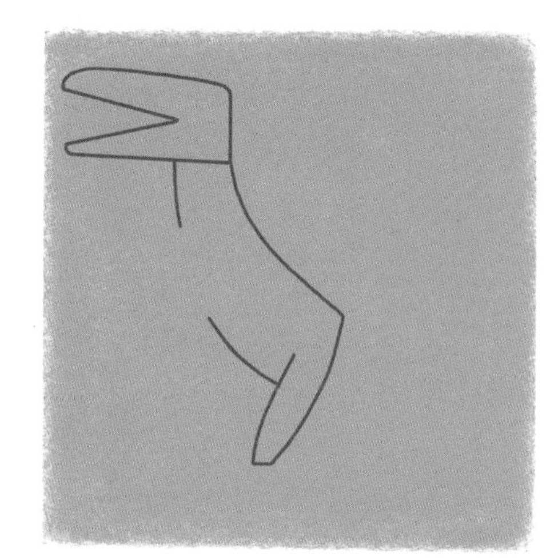

2 Add this shape for his body and one of his legs.

3 Then draw his other leg and his arm. Add his long tail and head crest.

4 Finish his legs. Give him lots of teeth and a little eye. He has feathers and claws on his arm!

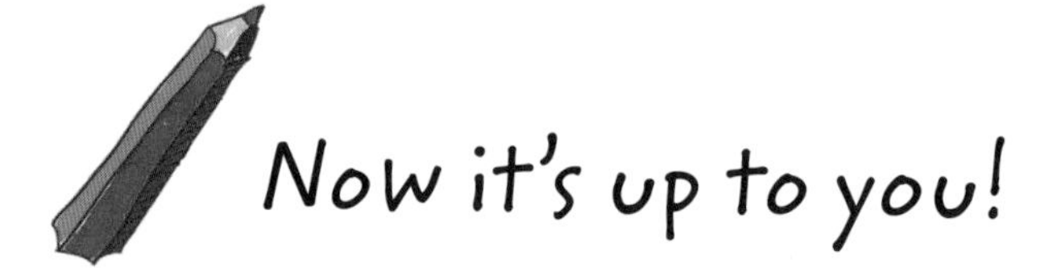

Now it's up to you!

Draw some Troodons hunting at night.

Draw a Pterodactyl.

Try drawing a Pterodactyl here.

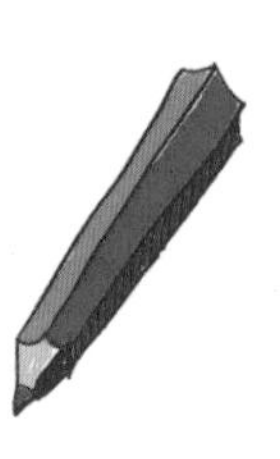

How many different dinosaurs can you draw?

Now try an Archaeopteryx.

1 Begin with the body of your Archaeopteryx (ARK-ee-OPT-er-ix).

2 Add her feathery wings.

3 Draw her head and long neck. Add some tail feathers and legs.

4 She has a face like a bird and little red feet.

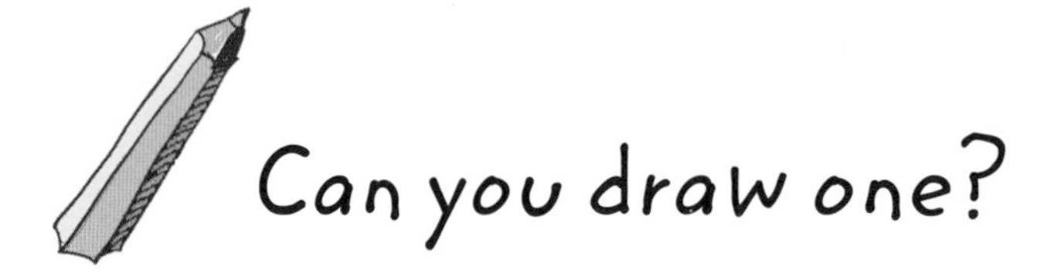

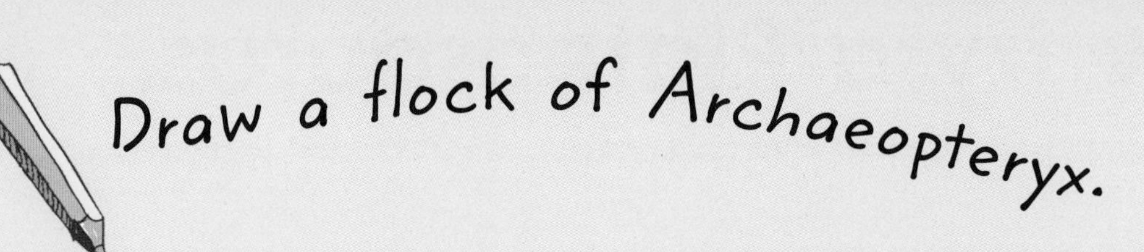
Draw a flock of Archaeopteryx.

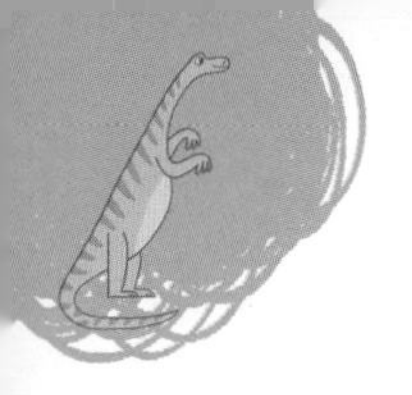

Now try a Plateosaurus.

1 First, draw the small head and long neck of your Plateosaurus (PLAT-ee-oh-SORE-us).

2 Now draw his body and one of his short front legs.

3 He needs a long tail and a strong back leg.

4 Add his other legs, and draw a happy face. Give him bright stripes from his neck to the tip of his tail.

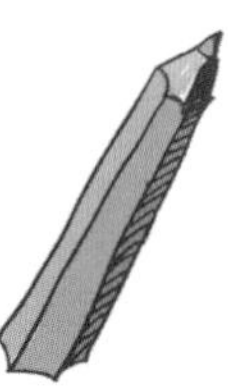

Draw your Plateosaurus here.

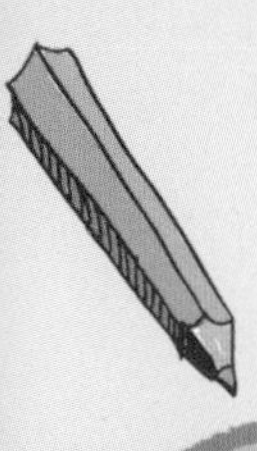

Draw a Plateosaurus going for a swim!

Now draw an Elasmosaurus.

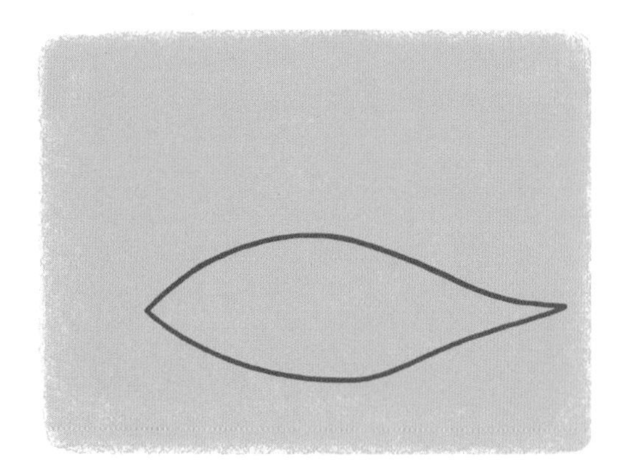

1 Begin by drawing the body of the Elasmosaurus (el-LAZZ-moh-SORE-us).

2 Add her four flippers.

3 She has a really long neck with a tiny head!

4 Finish by adding her face and some pretty stripes.

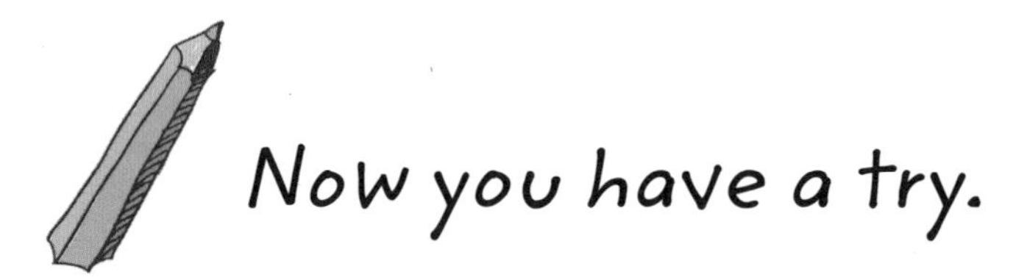

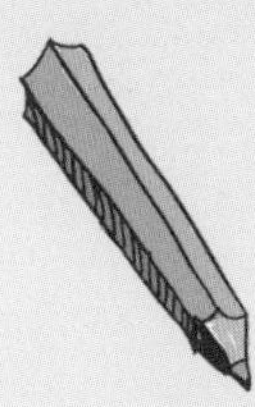

Draw an Elasmosaurus coming up for air ...

What about a Stegosaurus?

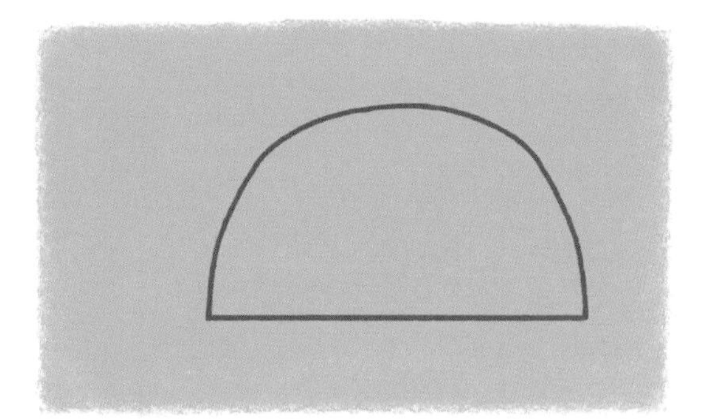

1 Her body has a nice rounded shape.

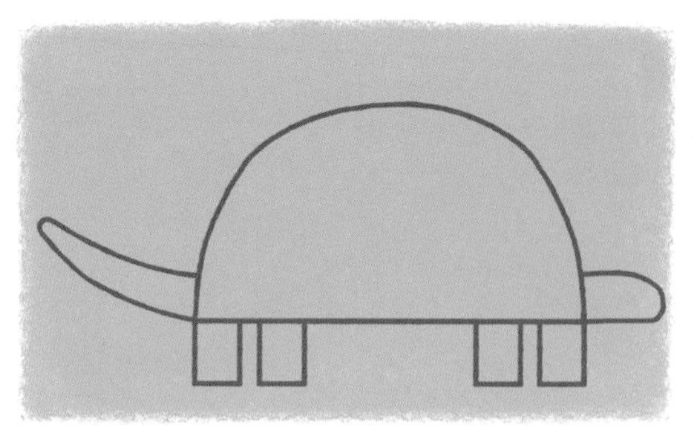

2 Add some short legs, a small head, and a tail.

3 She has lots of kite-shaped plates along her back.

4 Give her a happy face, bright spots, and some spikes on her tail!

Now you have a try.

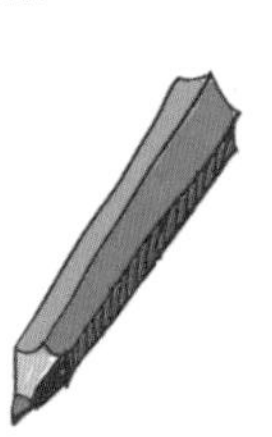

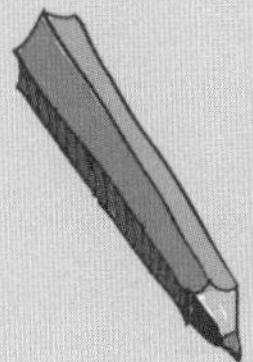

Can you draw the Stegosaurus that laid these eggs?

Let's draw an Iguanodon.

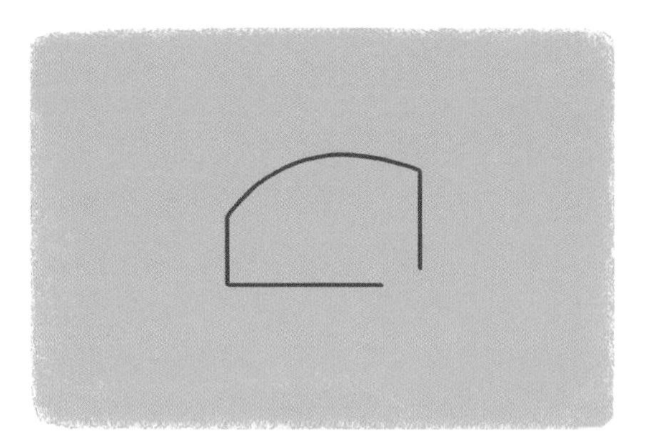

1 First draw the body of your Iguanodon (ig-WAH-noh-don).

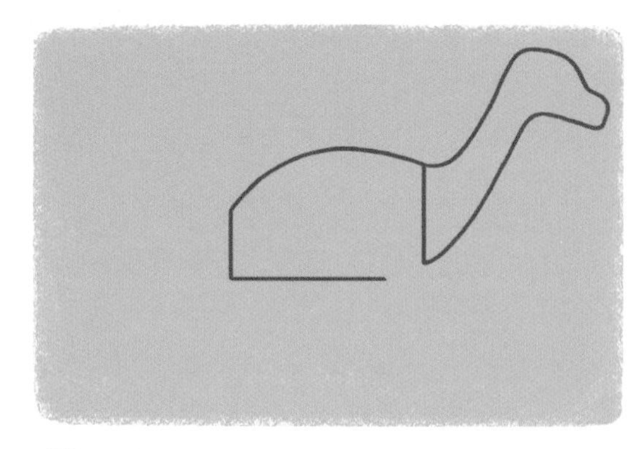

2 Then draw his head and long neck.

3 Now add his back legs.

4 He has short front legs, a long tail, and a sweet, beaky face.

Draw your Iguanodon here.

It's feeding time!

Draw some Iguanodons eating lunch.

Can you draw a Minmi?

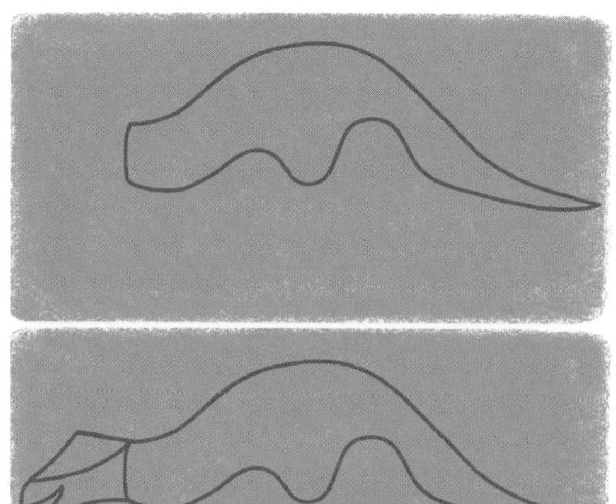

1 Start by drawing the body and tail of your Minmi (MIN-mee).

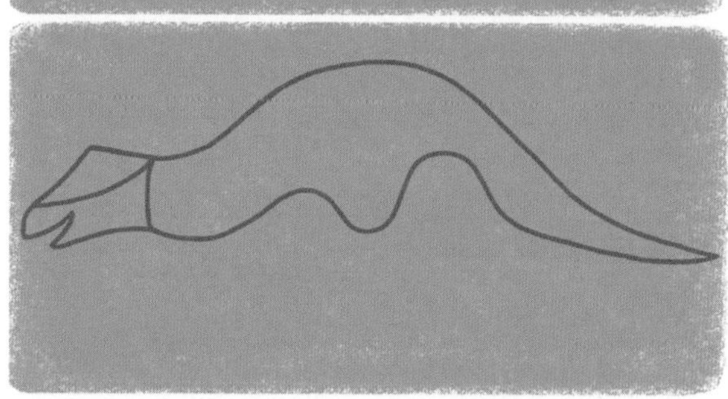

2 Draw her head. She has a hard plate on the top of her skull.

3 Now add her tummy and four legs. Draw three toes on each foot.

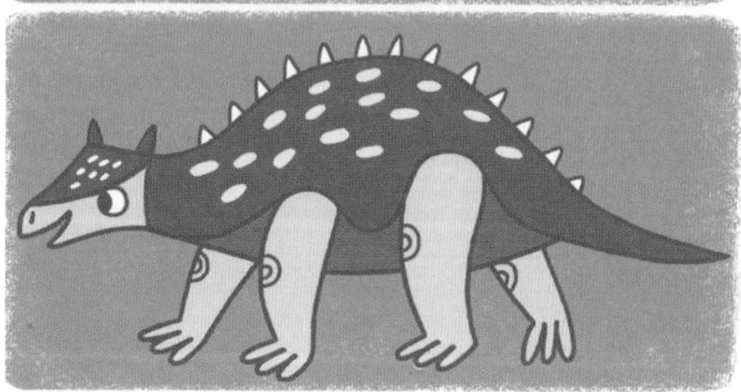

4 Give her a happy face and some small spikes along her back.

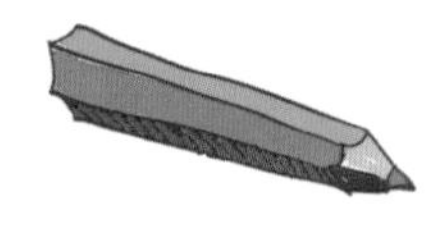

Try drawing a Minmi here. →

Draw some Minmis fleeing from the volcanoes!

On the Farm

Can you draw a goat?

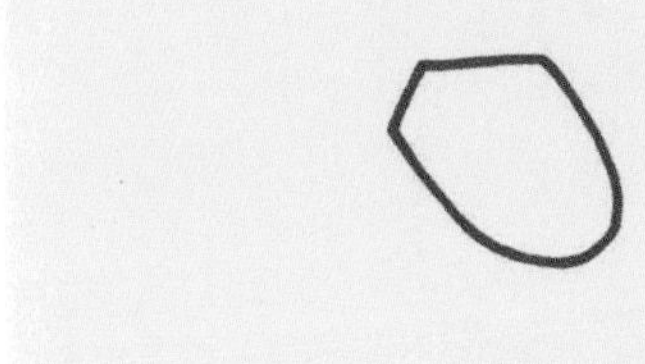

1 Here is her head.

2 Now draw her body.

3 Add her ears and legs.

4 Draw her face and two curly horns.

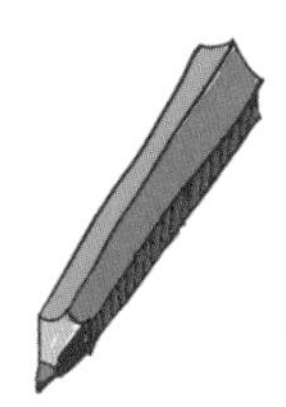

Draw some goats here.

What about a pig?

1 He has a nice round head and snout.

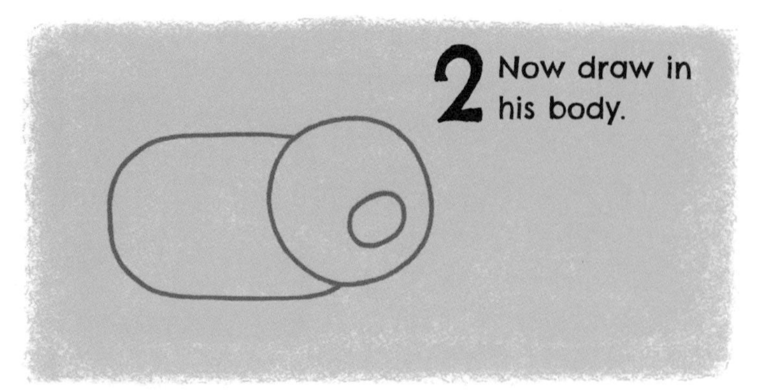

2 Now draw in his body.

3 He needs legs and ears.

4 Don't forget his face and his curly tail!

Try drawing a pig.

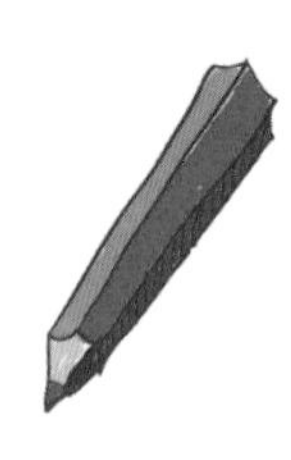

A farm needs a farmer!

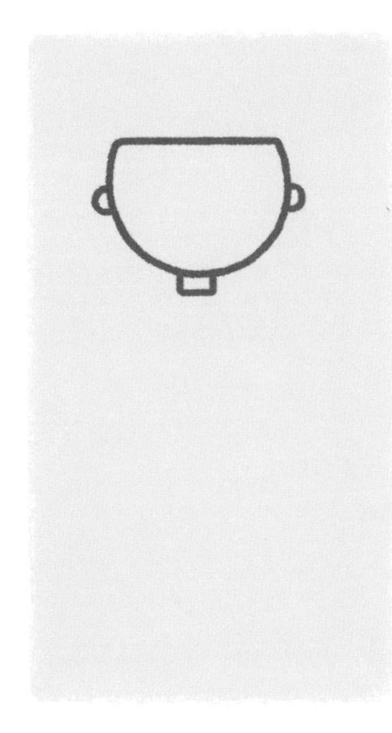

1 First draw his head.

2 Now add a body, arms, and legs.

3 He needs some clothes!

4 Give him a face and some smart red boots!

Try some different outfits:

Now you try!

Let's draw a tractor.

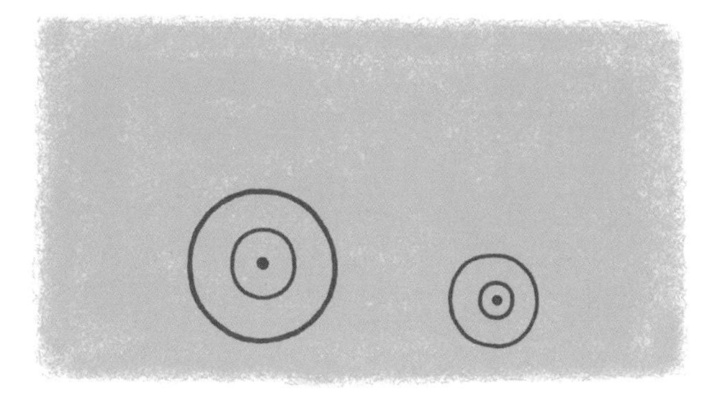

1 Draw the wheels—one big and one small.

2 Add the body and exhaust pipe.

3 The farmer needs somewhere to sit!

4 Make the tractor bright red.

Now it's your turn!

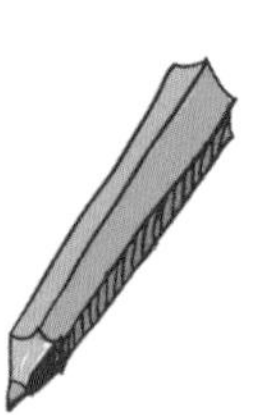

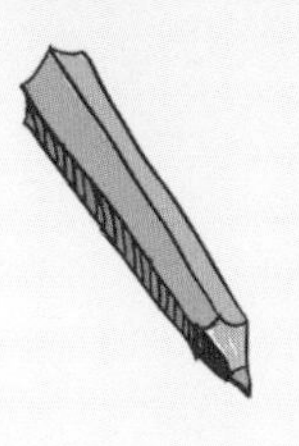

Draw a tractor on the hill.

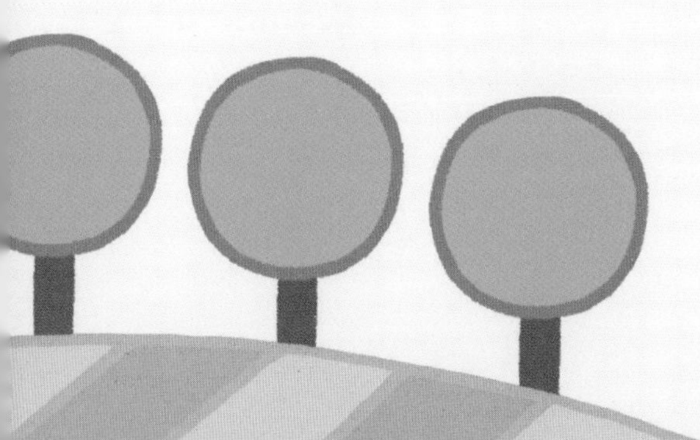

What animals are in the field?

Draw a happy sheep.

1 Let's start with his head.

2 Add his body and ears.

3 He needs legs and a little tail!

4 Give him a face and a thick, fluffy coat.

Now you have a try.

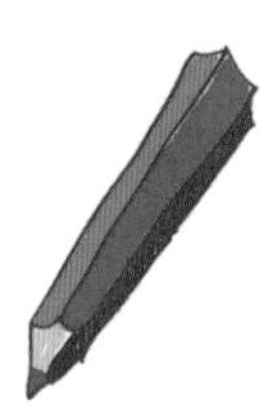

How many sheep are in the field?

Let's draw a chicken.

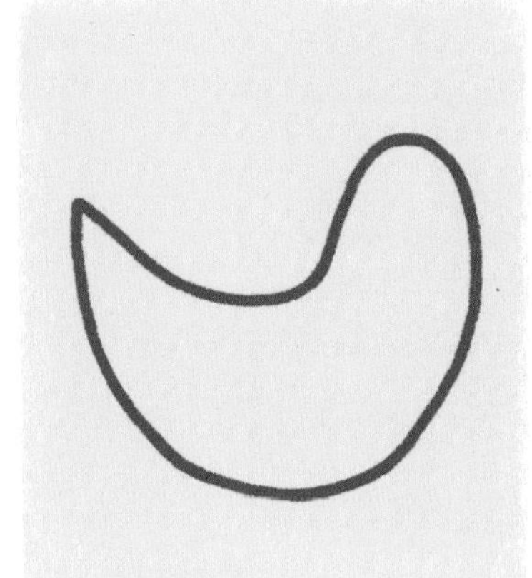

1 This is her body and head.

2 Add her beak and feathers.

3 Don't forget her legs and wing.

4 Draw her eye and feet. She's bright orange!

Try drawing some chickens here!

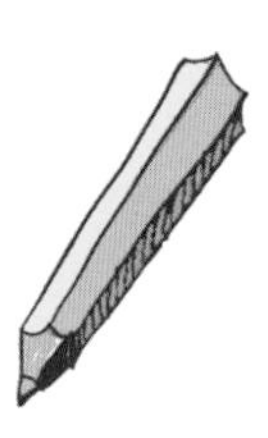

Draw some chickens around the hen house.

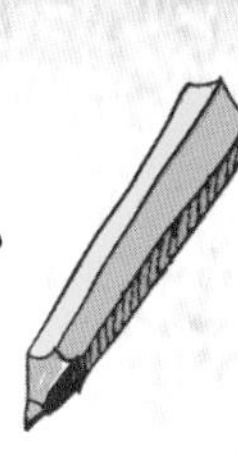

Have they laid any eggs?

How about a cow?

1 She has a large head and ears.

2 Add her horns. Her body is quite square.

3 She needs legs and a tail—almost finished!

4 Add her face and her pretty patches.

Now see if you can draw a cow.

Can you draw some animals in the farmyard?

Let's draw a duckling.

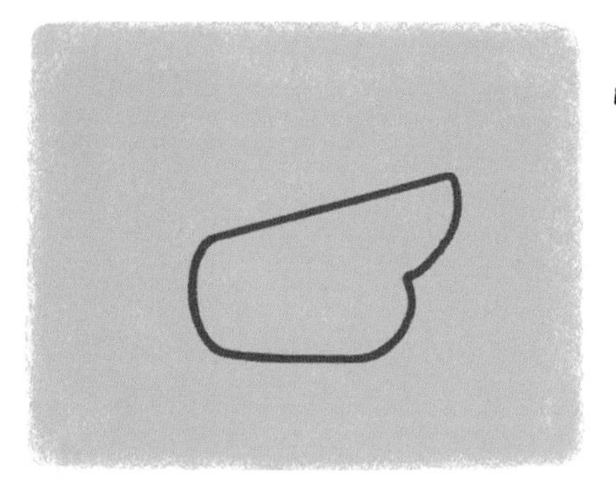

1 Start with this shape for the duckling's body.

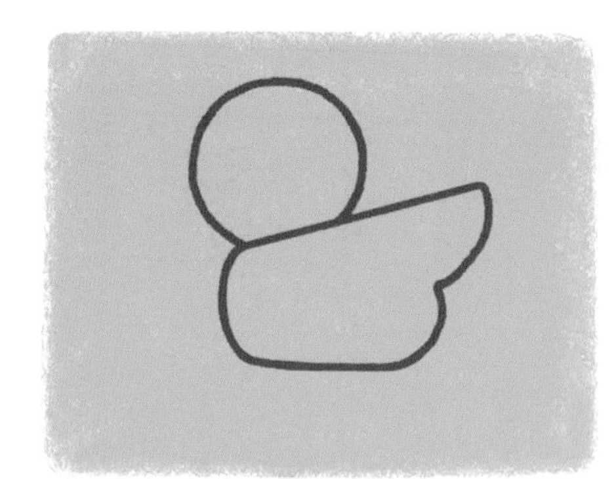

2 Add a round head on top.

3 He needs a beak and two little webbed feet!

4 Give him an eye and a wing. He has bright yellow feathers.

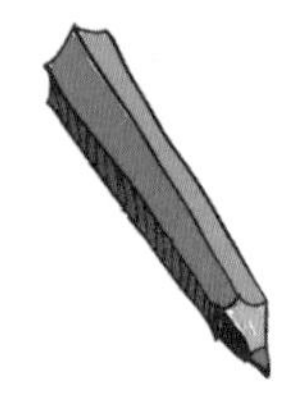

Draw some ducklings here:

Draw a line of ducklings following their mother.

Story Land

Let's start with a dragon!

1 Draw his long head.

2 Give him a body and ears.

3 Add shapes for his legs and wings—don't forget his tail!

4 Draw his face and feet, and make him green. Does he look fierce?

Draw your dragon here.

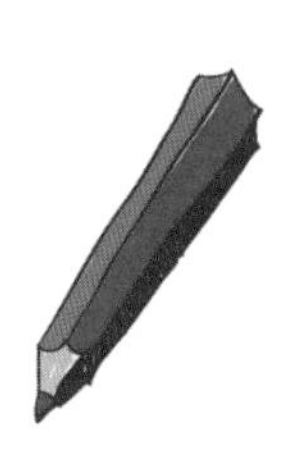

You will need a prince ...

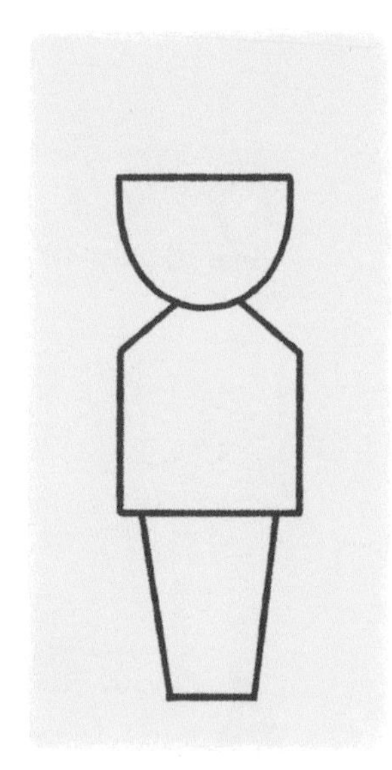

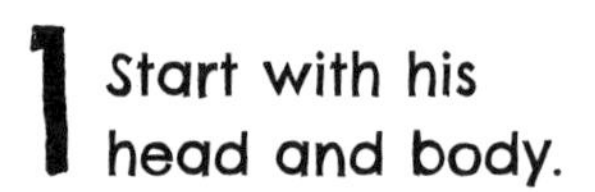

1 Start with his head and body.

2 Draw in his arms and legs.

3 Don't forget details like his crown!

4 He looks very handsome.

Try drawing a prince.

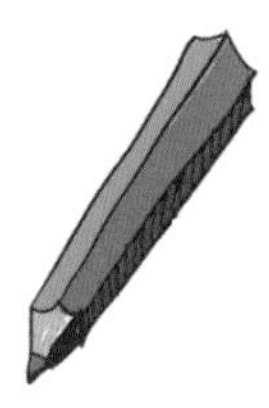

... and a princess!

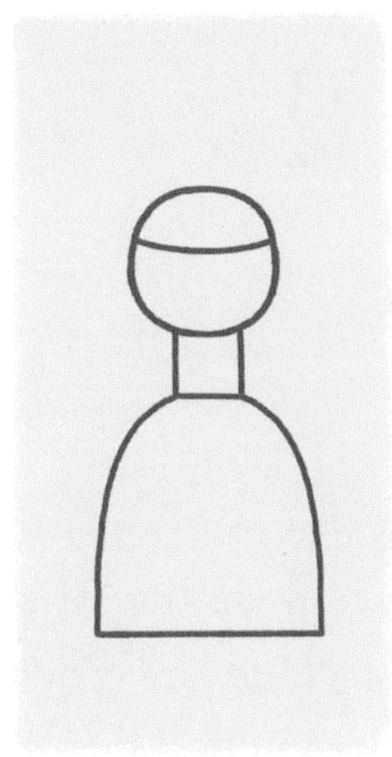

1 Draw her body and give her a round head.

2 She needs a long dress.

3 Draw her long, pretty hair and arms.

4 Add her face and crown. Now she's ready for the ball!

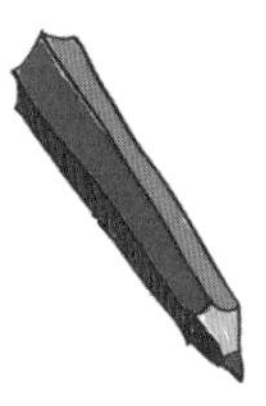

Use different crayons ...

Can you draw a unicorn?

1 First draw his body.

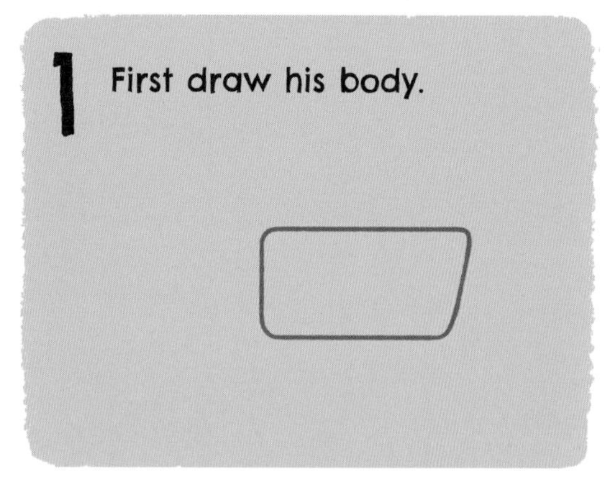

2 Then add his head.

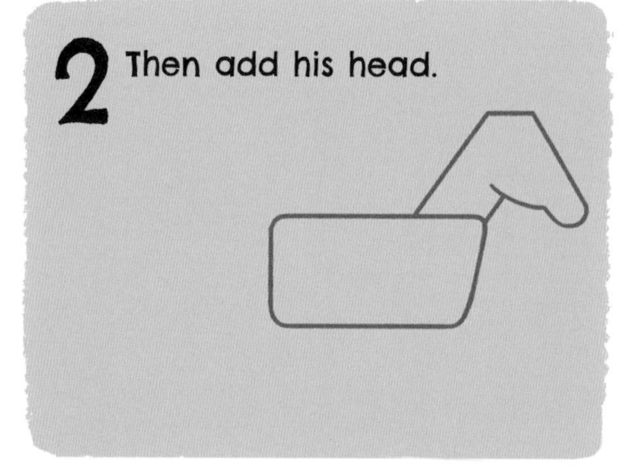

3 He needs ears and legs.

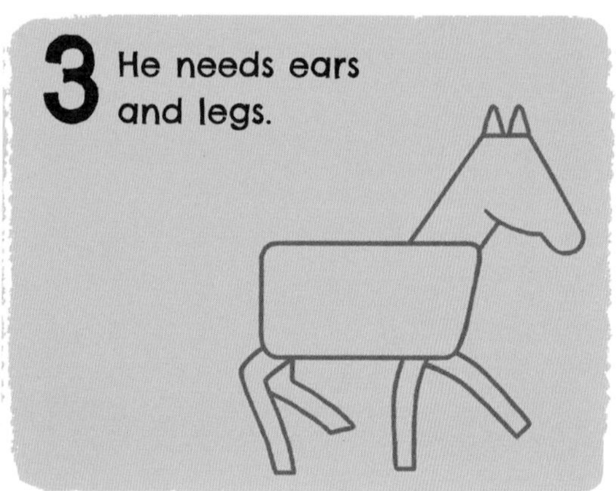

4 He has a pointy horn and a lovely tail!

Now you have a try!

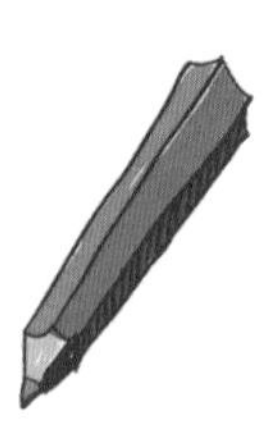

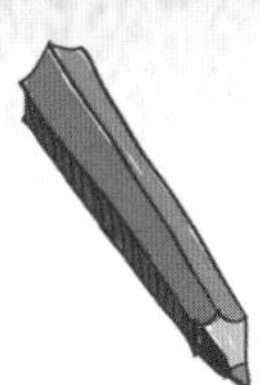

You can also draw other animals ...

A pony does not have a horn.

Give her a brown coat.

A pony with patches is called a piebald.

Pegasus is a flying horse. He needs some wings.

Draw a brave knight.

1 Let's start with his helmet.

2 He needs a shield.

3 Draw his tummy and arm.

4 Add his face, legs and sharp sword!

Now you try.

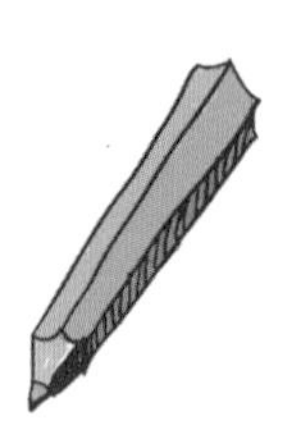

Can you draw some knights doing battle?

Let's draw a wizard.

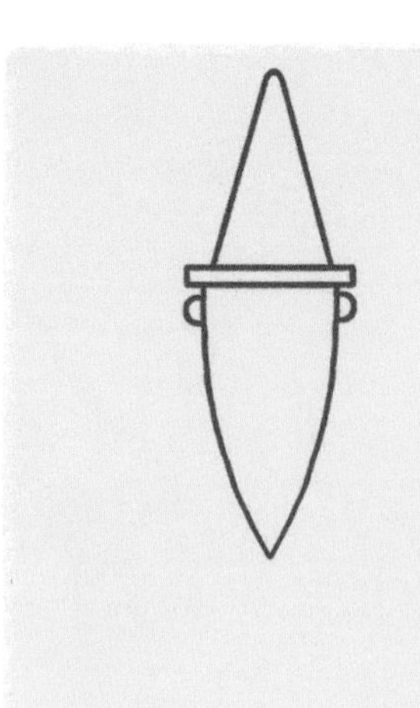

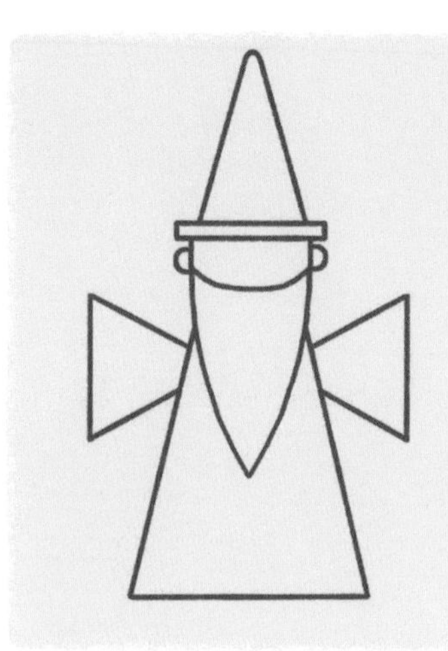

1 He has a tall, pointed hat ...

2 ... and a long, pointed beard.

3 Draw his long robe.

4 Add his face and cover him with moons and stars!

Try drawing a wizard here!

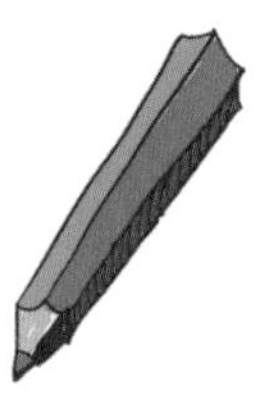

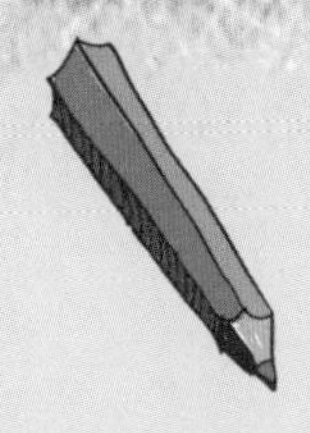

Draw a wizard casting a spell!

What kind of spell is it?

Draw a magical fairy.

1 First draw her head and dress.

2 She has a pretty hairstyle.

3 Every fairy needs legs and wings, of course!

4 Add her arms, and don't forget her wand! She has a pink dress and blue wings. What else?

Can you draw a fairy?

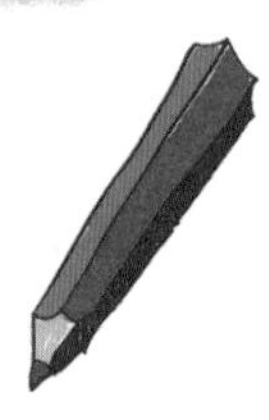

Draw a fairy godmother.

1 First draw this shape for her head and hair.

2 Add her pointed hat and two circles under her head—these are the tops of her sleeves.

3 Now draw her arms and dress.

4 Add her face and legs. She also needs wings ... and don't forget her magic wand!

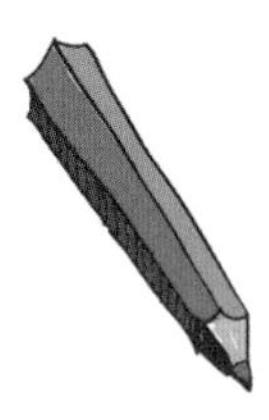

Try your fairy godmother here.

Can you draw a genie?

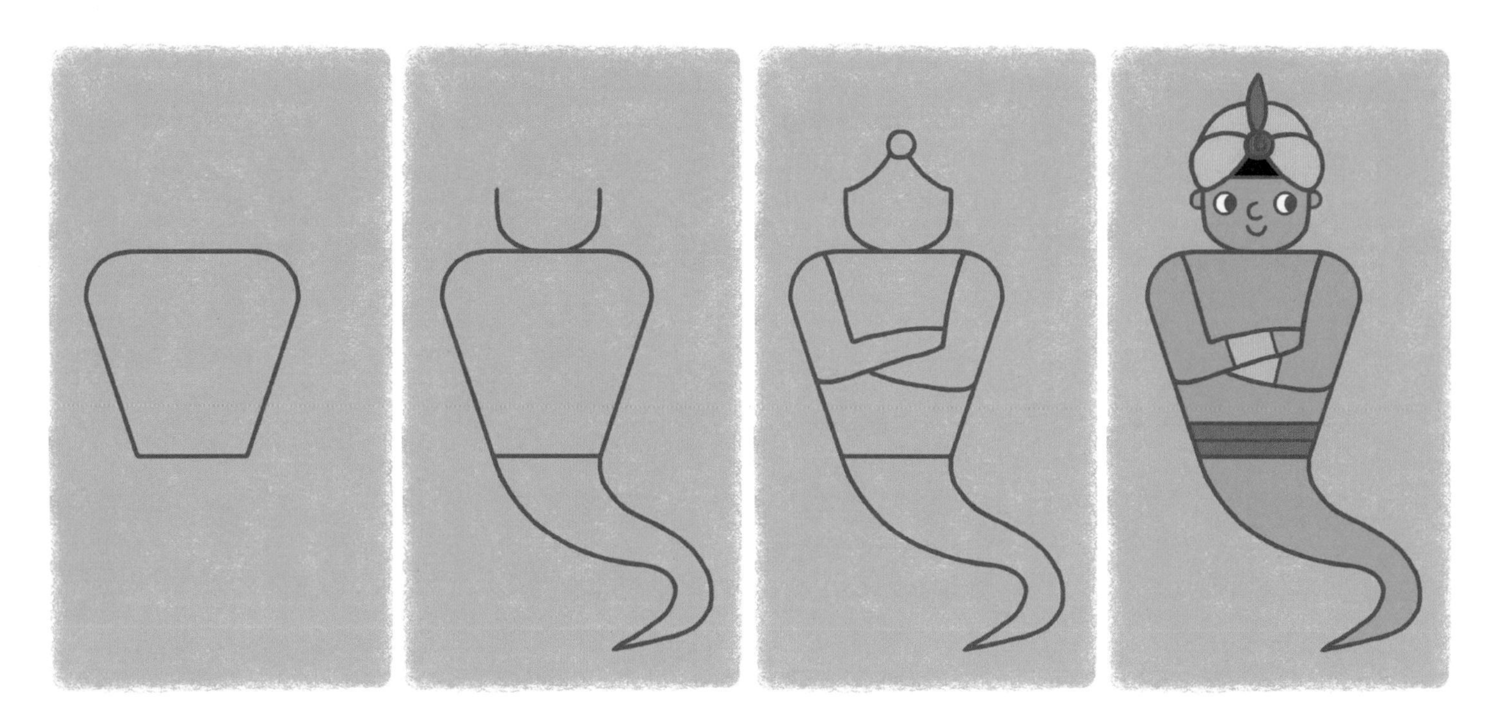

1 Start with this shape for the genie's body.

2 Add his face at the top and his wispy trail at the bottom.

3 Draw a jewel in the middle of his turban. His arms are folded.

4 Finish his turban. Add a belt and cuffs on his arms. He has a happy face.

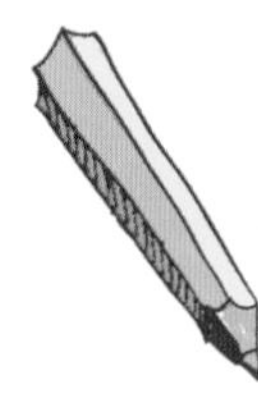

Now see if you can draw a genie.

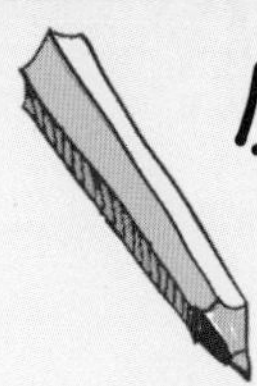

Draw a genie emerging from the lamp.

What about a mermaid?

1 Let's start with her head and the top of her outfit. Start drawing her hair.

2 Finish drawing her long flowing hair, and add her arms and hands.

3 She has a beautiful long tail!

4 Draw her face and some scales on her tail. Make her hair yellow and her tail green.

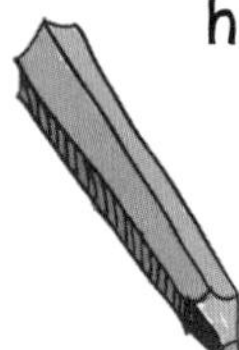

Now it's your turn!

Can you draw a mermaid under the sea?

Let's draw Puss in Boots ...

1 First draw this shape for his head and ears.

2 Now draw his body and arms. His right arm is pointing upward.

3 He needs a fluffy tail, a stylish hat, and some boots, of course!

4 Draw his face and put a feather in his hat. Make his hat black, his boots brown, and his fur orange.

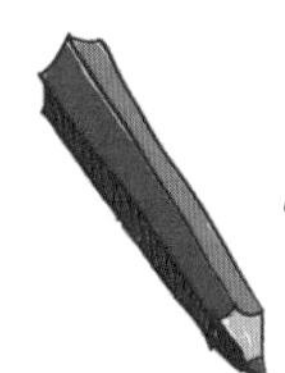

Now you can try.

... and Little Red Riding Hood!

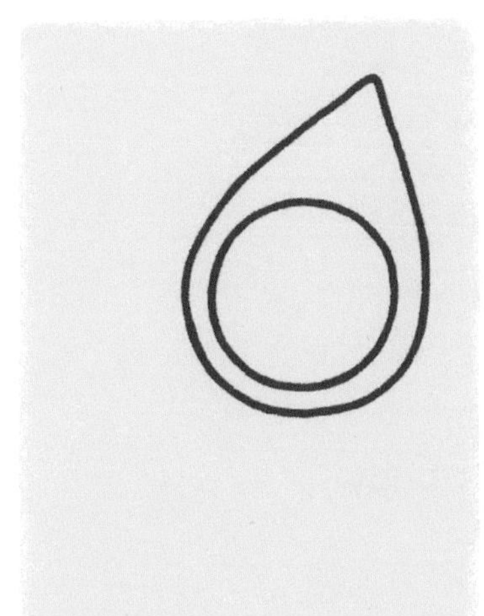

1 Let's start by drawing the pointed hood around her face.

2 Now draw her coat and arms.

3 Add her legs and boots. She needs a basket to take to Grandma's.

4 Draw her face and hair, and finish off her coat. Her outfit should be bright red, of course!

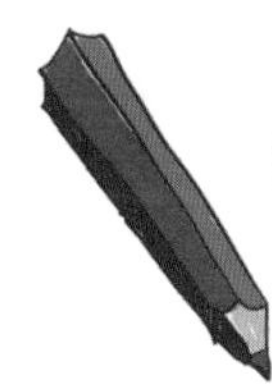

Can you draw her here?

Now draw the Big Bad Wolf!

1 Begin by drawing this shape for the wolf's head.

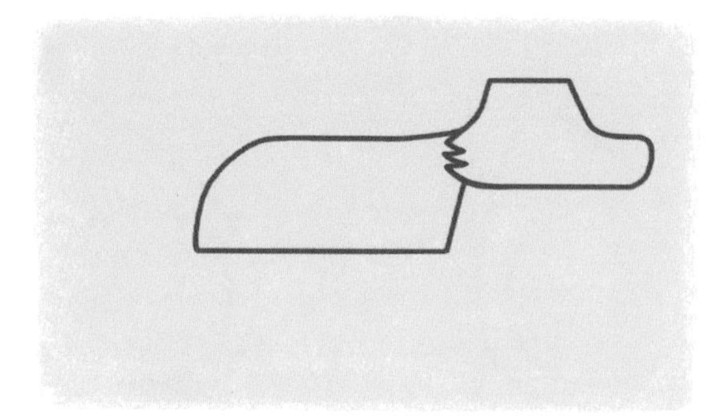

2 Now draw his body.

3 He needs four long legs.

4 Add his bushy tail, face, and ears. Shade in his fur.

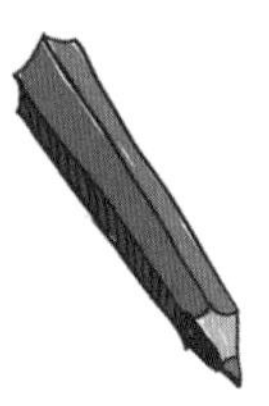

Try drawing the Big Bad Wolf here.

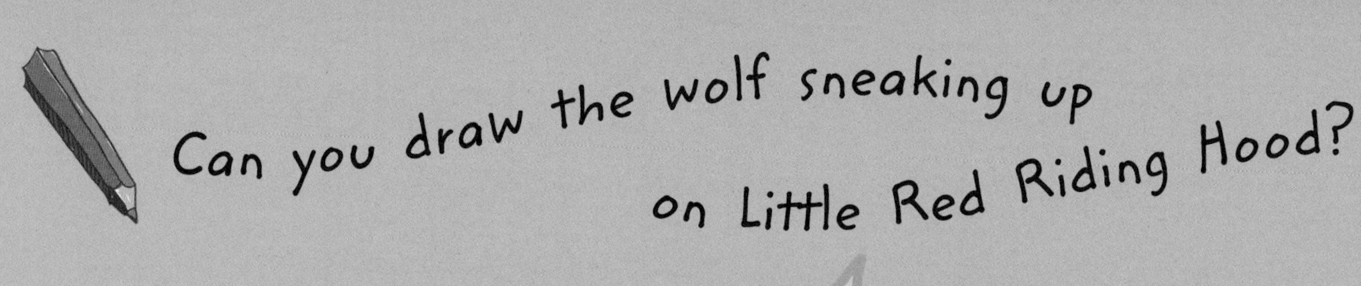

She's on her way
to Grandma's!

What about Dracula?

1 Start with Dracula's head. Make it flat at the bottom.

2 Draw a square for his body and add his high collar.

3 Draw his legs and feet. His arms point upward.

4 Draw his face, hair, and cloak. Don't forget his fangs! Make him black, purple, and red.

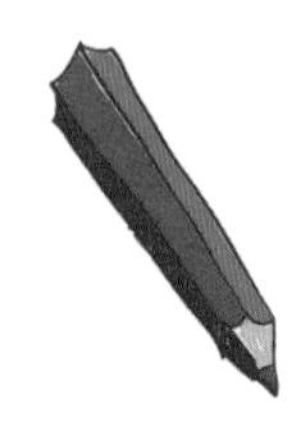

Draw your Dracula here.

Draw Dracula on the way to his castle.

Draw the wicked witch!

1 Start with her head and add her triangular dress.

2 Add her arms, hair, and ears. She needs a brim for her witch's hat!

3 Now finish her hair and pointy hat. Draw her legs and feet, and a broomstick in her hand.

4 Finish her broomstick. Draw her face and stripy socks, and shade in all her details.

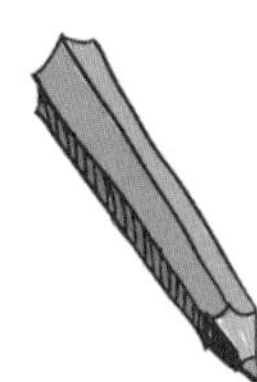

Draw a witch here.

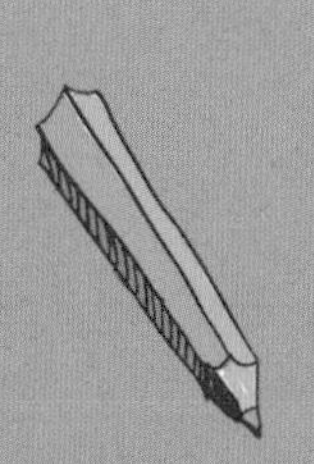

Draw some witches flying across the night sky.

Now draw a troll.

1 To start, draw a circle for the troll's head.

2 Then draw his big ears and the top part of his body.

3 Add his huge nose, and draw his arms, legs, and belt.

4 Give him some hair and make him a gross shade of green, with brown trousers and a black belt!

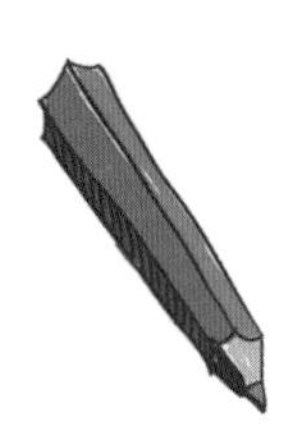

Now try drawing a troll.

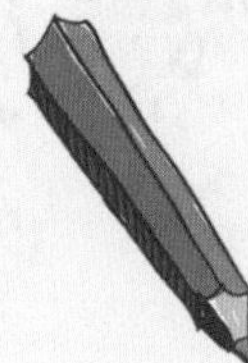

Can you draw some different trolls here?

Draw Dr. Frankenstein's monster.

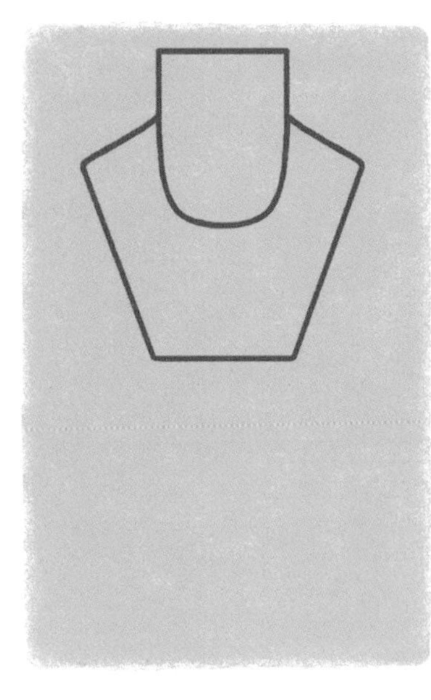

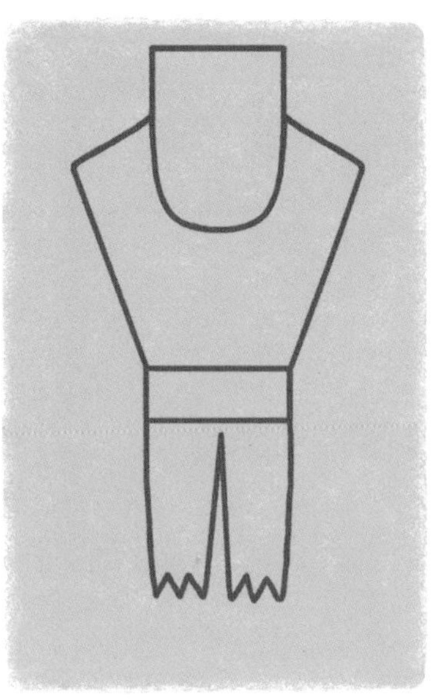

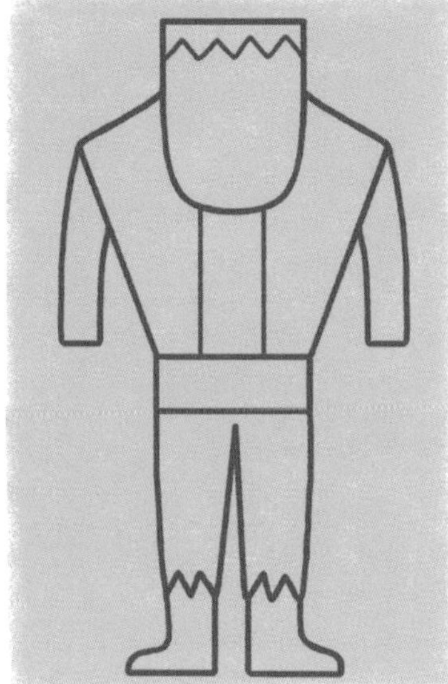

1 Start with these shapes for his head and body.

2 Now draw his belt and ragged trousers.

3 Add his arms and feet. Draw his hair and the edges of his coat.

4 Draw his face and hands. Don't forget the bolt in his neck and the scars on his face!

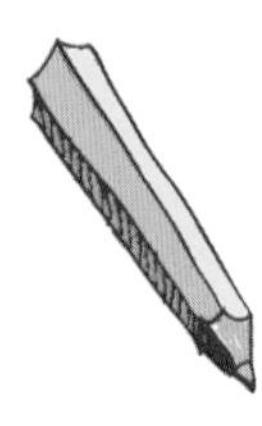

Draw your monster here.

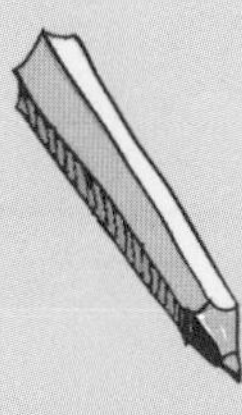

Draw a monster chasing Dr. Frankenstein!

Christmas

Can you draw Santa?

1 First draw his head. He has a long beard, and a small nose and ears. Add the fur around his hat.

2 Now finish off his hat and draw the top half of his body.

3 Draw his tummy and legs. His arms are open wide!

4 Add his face, belt, and boots. His outfit is red with a white trim and his mittens are green.

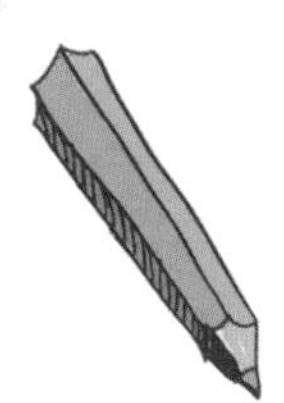

Now you try!

What about an elf?

1 Start with his head. Add some hair and his big, pointed ears.

2 Draw his tunic, one of his arms, and both his legs.

3 He needs a pointed hat with a bell and pixie boots. Draw a square for his gift.

4 Add his face and a belt. Draw a ribbon on his gift. He's dressed in green. Don't forget his stripy socks!

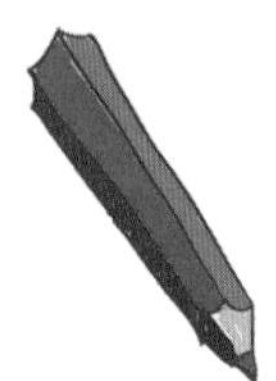

Try drawing an elf here.

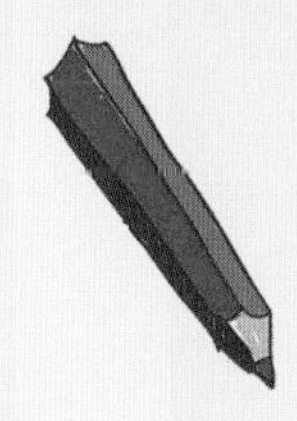

Draw some elves at work in the toy factory.

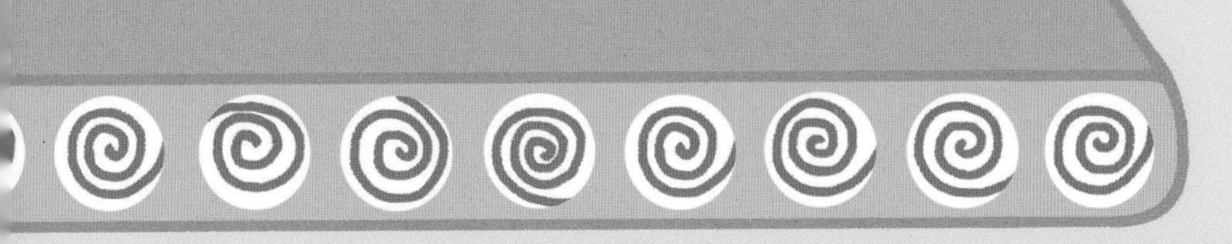

Draw a reindeer.

1 Start with the reindeer's head. She has small ears and a round nose.

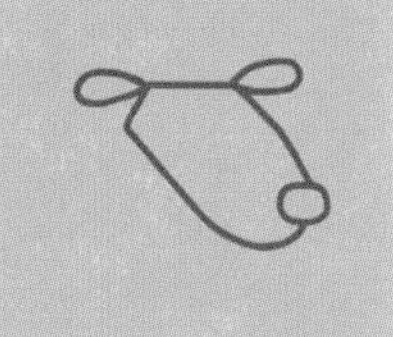

2 Now draw this shape for her body and a little tail.

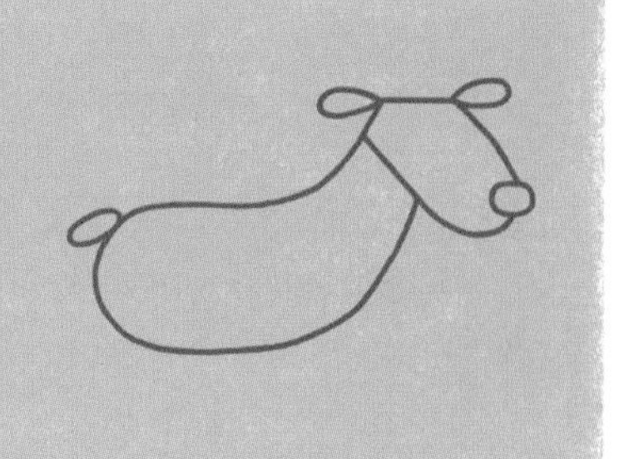

3 Add her collar and draw her legs so that she is running.

4 Draw her face and antlers. Shade her in—don't forget her red saddle!

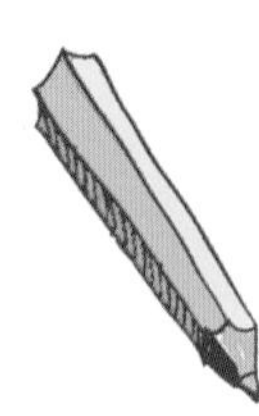

Draw a reindeer here.

Remember, only Rudolph has a red nose!

Can you draw all of Santa's reindeer?

Now draw Santa's sleigh!

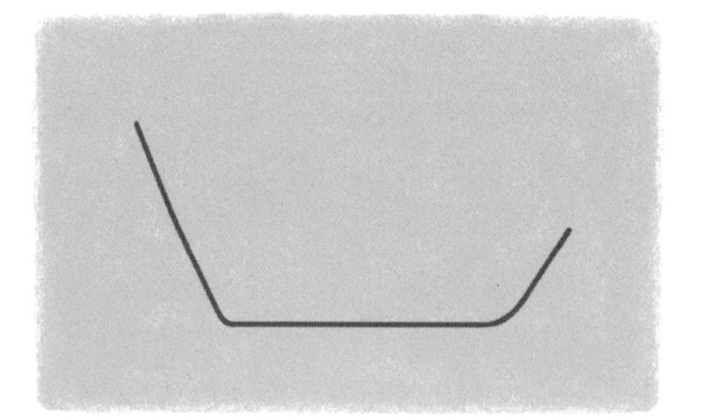

1 First draw three straight lines like this.

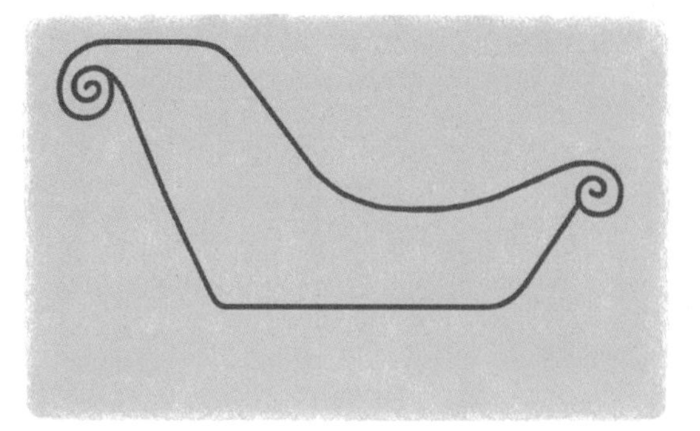

2 Then draw a curly line across the top.

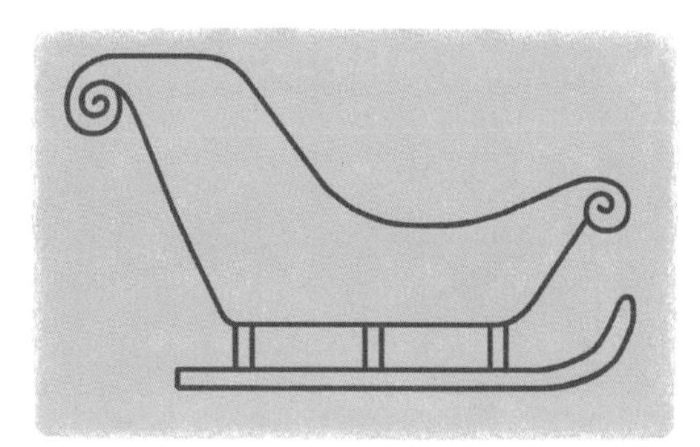

3 Add the runner at the bottom of the sleigh.

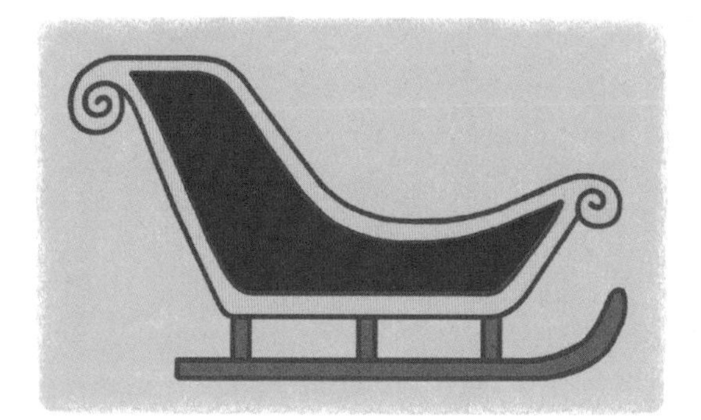

4 The sleigh is red and gold, and the runner brown.

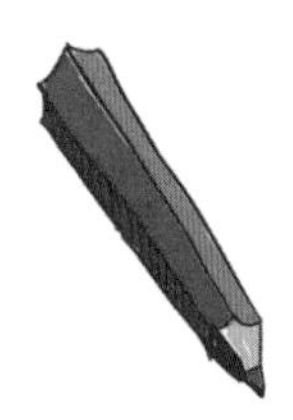

Now it's your turn!

Don't forget Mrs. Claus!

1 Start by drawing her head, hair, and ears.

2 Draw her dress, with fur at the bottom and around her hat. Draw the bun in her hair.

3 Complete her hat, and add her arms and legs.

4 Finish off her outfit and draw her face. Make her look neat in her red outfit.

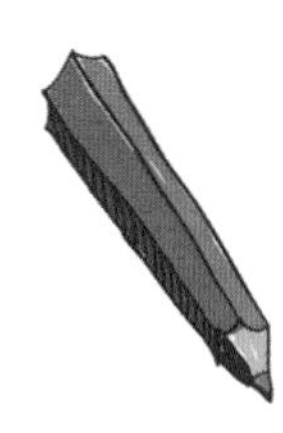

Try drawing Mrs. Claus here.

Draw a snowman.

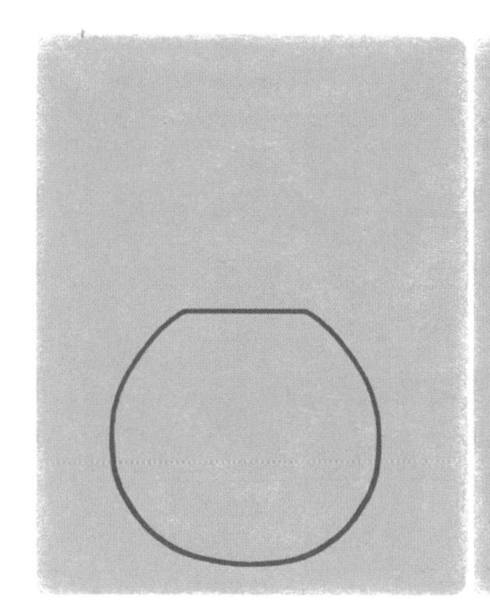

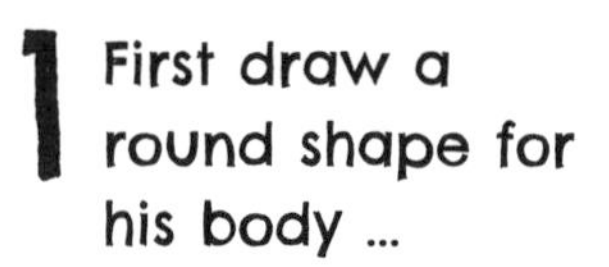

1 First draw a round shape for his body ...

2 ... and a smaller round shape for his head. Add the brim of his hat and a scarf.

3 Draw the top of his hat. Add his carrot nose and the ends of his scarf.

4 Finish by adding his face, some smart buttons, and twiggy arms. Shade in the details.

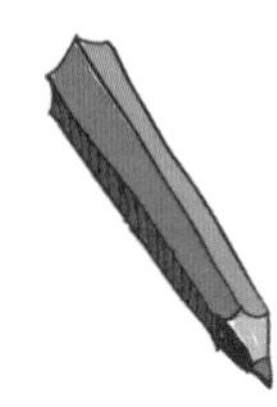

Now you draw a snowman!

Try one with a bobble hat ...

... or a black bowler hat.

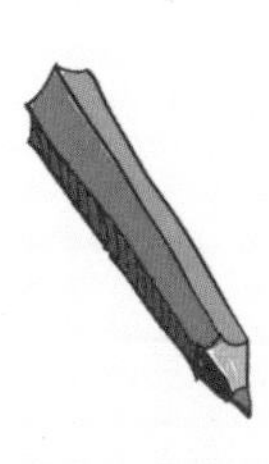

You can draw lots of different snowmen here.

Happy drawing!